MODI

FROM VISION TO REALITY

MODI
FROM VISION TO REALITY

R K Pachnanda

PENTAGON PRESS LLP

First published in 2023 by

PENTAGON PRESS LLP
206, Peacock Lane, Shahpur Jat
New Delhi-110049, India
Contact: 011-64706243

Typeset in Adobe Garamond, 11.5 Point
Printed by Aegean Offset Printers, Greater Noida, U.P.

ISBN: 978-93-90095-78-0 (HB)

www.pentagonpress.in

This book is dedicated to my respected parents,
Late Brigadier K.D. Pachnanda
and
Late Mrs. Bimal Pachnanda

CONTENTS

PREFACE

It is a great honour for India that, under the mantle of Prime Minister Narendra Modi, India has assumed the presidency of G20 in the momentous event at Bali. PM Modi's sterling and inspirational leadership was very much required by the world at this crucial juncture and moment for global change. His statement that today's era is not an era for war has been copied and quoted by many Heads of States. His statement that "Today's fertilizer shortage is tomorrow's food crisis" too became a quotable quote of the G20 Summit. His initiative of the International Solar Alliance and the concept of "One Sun, One Earth, One Grid" shall be followed by all nations.

Prime Minister Narendra Modi has set a new benchmark in reforms and governance for the world to emulate and has ably steered India to be one of the fastest growing economies of the world—stable and secure. He has a stellar status amongst the statesmen of the world today and is a true role model.

Within the country, PM Modi has taken unimaginable buoyant steps in every conceivable area. He has ensured "India First" in every policy formulation and execution. There has been a great leap forward in economic reforms, health care, serving the poor, Nari Shakti, ease of doing business, catapulting a tech-driven India, environment and sustainability and overall growth in all sectors. His devotion, grit and determination have rejuvenated and resurged India's unity, development and pride of a great new India.

PM Modi has brought "Vikasvaad" into the mainstream. His aim and efforts will enable India achieve 500 GW of green clean energy which will be a great boon and his gift to India and the whole world. The International

Energy Agency has called India's almost last-mile electrification the largest expansion of access within 1,000 days.

The patriotic and deft manner in which the Prime Minister led and guided the country during the COVID-19 catastrophe has been unparalleled and also emulated by many countries in the world. India's commitment towards the global community, highlighted several times by PM Modi's repeated assertion of "Vasudhaiva Kutumbakam" (The world is one family), as a guiding principle for our foreign policy, took shape in the most profound form in the form of the "Vaccine Maitri" campaign. India had the largest vaccination programme in the world and, as the "pharmacy of the world", supplied medical equipment, pharma products and vaccines to several countries, saving millions of lives across the world. During this period, India ran the largest food security programme for the poor. The Ayushman Bharat—Pradhan Mantri Jan Arogya Yojana—is the world's largest health insurance programme.

The global COVID-19 pandemic since 2020 had a severe economic fallout and jolted all countries across the globe. While many economies continue to struggle with sluggish economic growth and record- breaking inflation, India has been recognised, by global institutions like the IMF and World Bank, to be one of the fastest growing economies among the nations of the world—"a bright spot on this otherwise dark horizon."

The government's Aatmanirbhar Bharat plan turned the crisis into an opportunity and gave the much-needed impetus to economic growth. Under PM Modi's leadership, India is taking giant strides on all fronts. Several economic reforms have taken place since 2014. Inflation since 2015 has been under control. After the enactment of the Indian Bankruptcy Code, major cases of loan default have been resolved expeditiously. The introduction of GST proved to be of immense benefit to both consumers and business and has also reduced the scope and incentive for tax evasion. Following the Prime Minister's maxim of "Minimum Government, Maximum Governance", the Modi government has not only allowed privatising government businesses but also permitted the private sector to compete in areas where public sector presence may continue. Priority has been given to improving the infrastructure; enacting the Real Estate Regulatory Act has protected the middle class. Faceless tax assessment has reduced corruption. Programmes to reduce pollution, the Swachh Bharat Programme and making India ODF are some of the other progressive reforms which have taken place. The Pradhan Mantri Awaas Yojana, PM Kusum, the Ujjwala Yojana, Ujala, Deen Dayal Upadhyaya Gram Jyoti Yojana, introduction of Aadhar, Pradhan Mantri Jan Dhan Yojana (PMJDY), Pradhan Mantri Avas Yojna, Jal Jeevan Mission for safe and adequate drinking water, labour law reforms and innumerable other steps, schemes and missions, have provided great relief to the populace. Under the Business Reforms Active Plan, over 300 reforms across 70 action points for state governments, to develop an investor friendly eco system, have been introduced.

These last eight years have witnessed a paradigm shift in public service delivery and the implementation of government schemes and infrastructure projects. The government has ensured irreversible empowerment for various marginalised groups, helping them become self-reliant by providing a social safety net. The Government has launched the Startup India Seed Fund in accordance with PM Modi's true belief that "this world of startup reflects the spirit of new India".

PM Modi's active monitoring has made the infrastructure turnaround possible—be it highway construction, rapid increase in the construction of rural roads, a massive capacity expansion in the railways and metro rail in the last eight years or building or operationalising 66 airports and ensuring air connectivity to innumerable tier-2 and tier-3 cities. Digital connectivity and IT infrastructure have become critical determinants of our economic growth. Digital transactions will soon cross cash payments due to the increasing popularity of the Unified Payment Interface (UPI). The Cross Border Real Time Payment System connectivity too has been set up. India also aims to establish a place globally in the semi-conductor and electronics value chain. Further, emphasis is being given on the use and advancement of artificial intelligence. Recently the Modi Government approved the National Quantum Mission and became the sixth nation to join this venture.

Over the last eight years, India has emerged as a global leader on the issue of climate change. From negotiations over global climate change to the adoption of renewable energy, India is leading international efforts for environmental protection and shaping the global agenda since COP 21.

It has only been due to the vision, wisdom and sterling leadership of Prime Minister Narendra Modi that the security scenario in the country has improved dramatically. On the security front, Modi 2.0 envisions transformation of India into a new strong India—strong, secure, prosperous and invincible - an Aatmanirbhar Bharat, Sashakt Bharat, Swabhiman Bharat and an Ekatma Bharat.

The creation of the two Union Territories of J&K and Ladakh has been the greatest momentous achievement since Independence. With government priority on development for the people, the two Union Territories are witnessing a spate of unhindered development as never before. This is evident by steps taken by the government in promoting grass root institutions, building infrastructure and generating employment – all leading to economic development. The Modi Government's noble intentions, unflinching resolve, stupendous projects and schemes have brought hope and succour to all citizens. It has launched an indomitable crusade against terrorism; sponsors of terror have been globally isolated and India has made terrorism a global issue. The policy of zero tolerance as terrorism has ensured a stable and secure nation.

It is only because of PM Modi that infrastructure on the border has been strengthened on all borders, especially the Indo-China border. His visit to Ladakh to motivate the soldiers was truly a reflection of the greatest leadership and will not only go down in the annals of history but has also sent a firm message and a show of solidarity of a united India.

The government has firmly and effectively tackled the issues of illegal migration, drugs-arms-human trafficking, smuggling, influx of fake Indian currency and activities of insurgent groups.

The Prime Minister's personal intervention has led to building up a sound disaster response and sustainable disaster resilient infrastructure and India has taken a lead role in organising partner-nations to be disaster resilient.

All this will prove how patriotically the Modi government has kept the citizen—who is an equal stakeholder in national security—secure against all kinds of threats, external and internal. Here lies the accomplishment of a determined government which wants India to be one and committed towards the welfare of its countrymen. All this is because PM Modi's religion is India and welfare of all Indians.

On the foreign policy front, India has taken successful initiatives in the Gulf region. The essence of PM Modi's foreign policy is India's national interest. We have a pro-active Act East Policy and our Indian Ocean outreach is commendable. There has been proactive Indian involvement in QUAD as also our role in the Shanghai Cooperation Organisation, COP 26 Summit, FATF, IONS, IORA, BIMSTEC, BBIN, Pacific Islands Forum Summit, India CARICOM meet, G-7 Summits and the UN. Indians stranded abroad were brought home through Vande Bharat, the largest evacuation exercise in history; 3,000 students were evacuated from Ukraine in Operation Ganga and 800 Indians, under operation Devi Shakti, from Afghanistan. India has always assisted neighbours in crisis and has reached out to neighbouring countries to have a shared growth and future with all.

It is these proactive policies of Prime Minister Modi on every front that have made India an example for the world to follow. So much so that even President Biden remarked, "...I thank you for your continuing commitment to making sure democracies deliver".

Hence, the world is fortunate to have Prime Minister Modi as a leading light of G-20 and the torch bearer of peace and development to, successfully, address matters like the Ukraine war, climate issues, global recession, food security, energy security, bridging the digital divide, global value chains and international peace and stability, in line with the summit's motto of "one Earth, one Family, one Future."

R K Pachnanda

Contributors

Manohar Lal is the Chief Minister of Haryana from Karnal constituency in the Haryana Legislative Assembly since 2014. He is a former RSS Pracharak.

General V. K. Singh is the Minister of State in the Ministry of Road Transport and Highways and Minister of State, Ministry of Civil Aviation, Government of India. He was the Chief of Army Staff from 31 March 2010 to 31 May 2012.

Meenakshi Lekhi is the Minister of State for External Affairs and Culture of India. She is a Member of Parliament from the New Delhi Parliamentary constituency. She has been a lawyer in the Supreme Court of India.

Dr. Bibek Debroy is a well-known author and eminent economist. He is presently Chairman of the Economic Advisory Council to the Prime Minister (EAC-PM), Government of India. He was a member of the NITI Aayog, Government of India. He was awarded the Padma Shri in 2015.

Amitabh Kant is India's G-20 Sherpa and Ex CEO NITI Aayog, Government of India. He has worked in important capacities in the Government of India and Government of Kerala. He was earlier Secretary, Department of industrial Policy and Promotion, Government of India and Chairman, Delhi Mumbai Industrial Corridor Development Corporation. Author of *Incredible India 2.0*, *Branding India: An Incredible Story* and *Made in India*, he has been a key driver of "Incredible India", "Make in India" and "God's Own Country".

Rajiv Mehrishi was the Comptroller and Auditor-General of India (C&AG) and Vice-Chairman of the United Nations Panel of External Auditors. He was the Home Secretary of the Government of India till 31 August 2015.

Prior to that, he was Finance Secretary, Government of India. Before his appointment as Home Secretary, Government of India, he was the Chief Secretary, Government of Rajasthan. He was awarded the Padma Bhushan, India's third-highest civilian award, in 2022 by the Indian Government. Recently he has written a book, *India 2022*.

Sujan Chinoy is the Director-General of the Manohar Parrikar Institute for Defence Studies and Analyses (MP-IDSA), New Delhi, since 2019. A career diplomat from 1981 to 2018, he held several important diplomatic assignments, including as Ambassador to Japan. A specialist on East Asia, China and politico-security issues, he is on deputation to the National Security Council Secretariat (NSCS) for many years. He is the Chair of the Think20 engagement group for India's G20 Presidency.

Harsh Vardhan Shringla is the Chief Coordinator of India's G20 Presidency. Prior to this, he was Foreign Secretary of India. He has been Ambassador to the United States of America, Thailand, and Bangladesh. He was also Consul-General of India in Durban, South Africa, and Ho Chi Minh City, Vietnam. He is an experienced multilateral diplomat, having worked on two UN Security Council tenures, has served in the Indian mission to the UN in New York and has also been Permanent Representative to UNESCAP.

Anil Wadhwa was Secretary (East) in the Ministry of External Affairs between 2014 and 2016. He served as Indian Ambassador to Italy, Thailand, Oman, and Poland. He has also served as the Indian Ambassador and Permanent Representative to FAO, IFAD, and WFP UNESCAP and worked with the Organization for the Prohibition of Chemical Weapons (OPCW) at The Hague, heading the Government Relations and Political Affairs, Media, and Public Affairs branches. Currently, he is a Distinguished Fellow in the New Delhi-based Vivekananda International Foundation.

Ajay Bisaria is a former career diplomat of the Indian Foreign Service. He served as High Commissioner of India to Canada and Pakistan, and Ambassador of India to Poland and Lithuania. He has also represented India at the World Bank in Washington DC and in embassies in Berlin and Moscow. He has served in various capacities in India and in the Ministry of External Affairs, Department of Commerce, and the Prime Minister's Office from 1999 to 2004.

Bharat Lal is Director-General, National Centre for Good Governance, Government of India. He is the founder-CEO of WASMO, Gujarat, and also founder-Mission Director, Jal Jeevan Mission, Government of India. He has worked as Secretary, Lokpal of India. Since March 2020, he also worked in the core team formed by the Government of India to manage COVID-19. He has also served as Additional Secretary to the former President of India.

Nalin Kohli is an advocate at the Supreme Court of India and national spokesperson of the BJP. He is also the senior Additional Advocate-General of the Governor of Assam, the government nominee of the Ministry of Corporate Affairs, Government of India and Chairman of the Anti-Doping Appeal Panel of the National Anti-Doping Agency (NADA). He is a well known media personality and has been the Founder-Director of a leading media institute, in collaboration with the Missouri School of Journalism, USA.

Maj-Gen Dhruv C. Katoch, SM, VSM is a third-generation officer from the Indian Army. He has been awarded the degree of Doctor of Philosophy (*honoris causa*) from the Indira Gandhi University, Rewari, in 2016. He has been Director of the Centre for Land and Warfare Studies (CLAWS), the Indian Army premier think-tank. He is presently, the Director, India Foundation.

Uttam Kumar Sinha is a Senior Fellow and Centre Coordinator of the Security Centre of the Manohar Parrikar Institute of Defence Studies and Analyses. He has been a leading commentator on trans-boundary water issues, climate change and the Arctic Circle. He is the Managing Editor of the Routledge published *Strategic Analysis*. He is currently the Co-Chair of the T-20 Task Force on "Accelerating SDGs" during India's G20 Presidency. He is a recipient of many fellowships and leadership programmes and has also written books. He regularly writes for the *Hindustan Times* and *Prabhat*.

Sanjay Tandon is a Chartered Accountant, President, UTCA and Member, National Council BJP. He is presently a Director, National Mineral Development Corporation, Member, Administrator's Advisory Council, Chandigarh Administration, Member, Bharat Vikas Parishad, Chandigarh;

Member, DAV Management Committee Pratinidhi Sabha and is holding other portfolios. He has been Director of State Bank of Hyderabad and the National Hydroelectric Power Corporation.

Maroof Raza is a well known media commentator on global, military and security issues. He has edited/co-authored: *Confronting Terrorism* and *Kashmir's Untold Story: Declassified* (published by Bloomsbury in 2019), and now *Contested Lands: India, China and the Boundary Dispute* (published by Westland/Amazon.com).

Satnam Singh Sandhu is the Founder and Chancellor of Chandigarh University, Founder-Chairman, Chandigarh Group of Colleges, Founder, Chandigarh Welfare Trust and Chief Patron, NID Foundation.

Shishir Bajoria is the Chairman, IIM Shillong, Core Committee Member, Videsh Vibhag BJP, In-charge, Media Relations, Member, Election Commission Dept. and State Executive, BJP West Bengal and Vice Chairman, Europe-India Business Council.

R K Pachnanda is currently the Chairman, Haryana Electricity Regulatory Commission. Prior to this he was Chairman, Haryana Public Service Commission, Security Adviser to the Chief Minister, Assam, Director General, Indo-Tibetan Border Police (ITBP), Director General, National Disaster Response Force (NDRF) and Commissioner of Police, Kolkata. He has also served in important capacities in the CBI, SPG, BSF, CRPF, and CISF. He has authored a book "Terrorism and Response to Terrorist Threat" and co-edited "Modi 2.0: A Resolve to Secure India".

1

A Strong and Stable India under Narendra Modi

Manohar Lal

The sterling leadership of Prime Minister Modi has led India towards a stable, self-reliant, and strong country with a high growth rate and development in the economy, health services, investment, ease of doing business and all other spheres. Prime Minister Modi has strengthened national security, and blended diverse aspirations and beliefs of the Indian people and channelized their collective determination to reinforce the pride of being an Indian in a confident and patriotic India. Emanating from the mantra of Vasudhaiva Kutumbakam and Sarvey Bhavantu Sukhina, the world has begun following India. The Prime Minister's focus on *Sabka Saath—Sabka Vikas—Sabka Vishwas* has taken development and prosperity to all the corners of the country. The mantra of "Minimum government, maximum governance" has yielded results and empowered millions of people at the grassroots level.

India is well poised to become the third-largest economy of the world by 2030. Prime Minister Narendra Modi's vision, planning, and attention to detail has led India in constantly moving towards prosperity. For this reason, India is one of the fastest growing economies in the world. Even the International Monetary Fund (IMF) has stated that in this difficult period,

India's position is better than others and is a bright spot on the otherwise dark horizon. Despite the COVID-19 catastrophe, the investment climate of the country has improved with focus on the ease of doing business. There has been a great metamorphosis following the new educational policy which will produce skilled manpower to cater for India's vibrant economy. All these measures reflect India's resolve to surge ahead as the Modi Government is committed to fulfil the dreams of all Indians.

The Prime Minister does not see reforms in a piece-meal manner but thinks big for a strong India. He feels that national encompasses economic strength, technological prowess coupled with powerful national consciousness along with military might. To achieve a stable and strong India, he followed various measures. The Foreign Investment Promotion Board was abolished and multiple sectors liberalized for FDI. GST was introduced subsuming 17 taxes and multiple cesses, creating a truly national market. With the passage of the Real Estate Regulatory Act (RERA), customer rights in the real estate sector have been protected. Digital payments were promoted in a big way so much so that India has become a world leader in the digital payments sector. The Prime Minister's efforts to create a world class digital financial infrastructure have been complemented by an active blend of government efforts and innovative steps taken by banks and fintech firms. The Government's role has emerged to be a facilitator of private sector-led development, following the Prime Minister's maxim of "Minimum government, maximum governance". With the great focus on making India an entrepreneurship and innovation hub, the Prime Minister personally drove the Start-up India Movement. Today, India has one of the most dynamic start-up ecosystems in the world.

The Prime Minister recognized the true potential of Aadhaar to be an effective instrument to deliver Government benefits. To ensure opening of bank accounts by the population, the Pradhan Mantri Jan Dhan Yojana (PMJDY) was launched. Riding on the triad of Jan Dhan Yojana, Aadhaar and Mobile (JAM), 13 lakh crore cumulative Direct Benefit Transfers (DBT) have been made. India is rapidly expanding its optical fibre network to ensure that every village is provided with high-speed internet connectivity. Through the Digital India Mission, a multitude of government services is now available to citizens through the online mode including the Government-e-Marketplace (GeM), the National Public Procurement portal. Multifarious initiatives have been taken to enable ease of living and access to basic amenities for all sections of society like Housing for all, 100 per cent electrification, launching of the Jal Jeevan Mission for safe and adequate drinking water, the Pradhan Mantri Grameen Sadak Yojana for rural road connectivity and release of new LPG connections for most of the districts and many other such initiatives to empower Indians for a new stable India.

Prime Minister Modi has displayed a positive and constructive approach, social sensitivity, and strong political will to make the impossible possible.

The road sector is playing a pivotal role in creating world-class infrastructure for India. This shall not only change the face of roads but also ensure a new and bright future for New India. The Swachh Bharat Mission became possible only due to the vision of the Prime Minister Modi. People's participation triggered the Swachh Bharat Jan Andolan, perhaps the biggest behavioural change movement ever, where a nation of a billion people demanded and worked for clean surroundings. Most districts of the country have witnessed immense transformation across sectors like health and nutrition, education, agriculture, financial inclusion and basic infrastructure because of the confluence of Central and State Government schemes and real-time monitoring of the progress in each district.

The other reforms undertaken by Prime Minister Modi are in bankruptcy law, labour law reform, simplification and reduction of corporate profit tax, ending the Indian Medical Council Act, 1956, social spending with the digital payment system and ease of living for citizens. Prime Minister Modi has done yeoman work in renewable energy and energy efficiency, water supply, sewage treatment, wildlife conservation, Clean India Mission and urban rejuvenation.

Recognizing new aspirations in Indians and seeing the availability of new opportunities, the Prime Minister launched the National Educational Policy which has brought in reforms in the education sector like digitization, critical thinking, integrated and inter-disciplinary learning with special focus on developing scientific temperament amongst students. Emphasis is on learning-driven education rather than rote marksheet-driven education.

There has been great progress and monitoring on space technology and Artificial Intelligence. The Prime Minister's efforts are to navigate India forward on the path of digital excellence in making India an Artificial Intelligence hub in the world. The National Programme on Artificial Intelligence is dedicated to ensure proper use of Artificial Intelligence to solve multiple development and challenges in agriculture, healthcare, climate change, and urbanization.

Prime Minister Modi has shown extraordinary willpower to protect India's digital frontiers as well. He took the bold step of banning outright certain mobile apps that were posing a threat to India's data sovereignty, defence, public order, and privacy of citizens. In the long term, Prime Minister Modi is working on creating a safe cyberspace, secure data privacy of Indians, and protect data sovereignty. Taking cognizance of the threats in the digital world, the government has prepared the National Cyber Security Strategy 2020 to make India a cyber-secure nation. The security aspects of the 5G roll-out have also been adequately addressed in the Strategy. To ensure inclusive growth and empowerment of the poor and underprivileged, hitherto neglected rural areas have been brought within the ambit of the digital world. Prime Minister Modi has implemented digital technologies for the welfare of common citizens of India. He has not shied away from taking a tough stand in the larger interests of the country and its people.

A group of former eminent civil servants with vision and experience has also shared their perspectives on the initiatives undertaken by Prime Minister Modi in different areas like foreign policy, internal security, health education, digital revolution, agriculture, defence and others.

The Prime Minister provided inspiring leadership of the highest order to manage and mitigate the COVID-19 crisis. He led from the front ensuring the active collaboration of technology, welfare reform and health care schemes and a forward-looking economic policy to prevent and contain the devastating effects of this global disruption. India launched the largest free food programme for 80 crore citizens and the largest vaccination programme in the world. Medical equipment and vaccines were sent to various countries to help them in times of need.

On foreign policy, the Prime Minister had displayed tremendous dexterity in ensuring that the country is fully protected and that India is an accepted global voice of the world. Prime Minister Modi's achievements on the international front in catapulting India to a different level flow with his ability to plan and effectively execute due to his vision in adapting to changed circumstances have been widely acclaimed. The crux of Prime Minister Modi's foreign policy is the unflinching pursuit of national interests with a willingness to go beyond the doctrinaire approach of the past. India does not let any country dictate anything contrary to its national interests or what our domestic policies should be. There is a refreshing new and proactive approach to the foreign policy that Prime Minister Modi has brought that demonstrates what a focused and strong leadership with the ability to deliver can achieve. Within the broader framework of India's Neighbourhood First policy, the Government has strengthened bilateral relations with all its neighbours. Timely assistance provided during the COVID-19 pandemic reflects the importance accorded by India to its neighbouring countries. India has successfully negotiated and signed a historic Land Boundary Agreement (BA) with Bangladesh to settle the decades-old boundary dispute. Proactive diplomacy with Russia, the USA, Japan, Australia, the UK, and France has created new vistas of cooperation. Engagement with West Asia, Central Asia, ASEAN, BIMSTEC, IORA, QUAD, and I2U2 has yielded positive results.

Prime Minister Modi has taken an active stand on international issues, following a bold and outcome-driven foreign policy. In his first three years in office, he visited fifty countries. His approach has always been "India First', due to which he engaged with partners despite rivalries or differences and who were convinced about his strong beliefs and sincere intentions. His personal conviction about India's role in the international system, its spiritual and civilizational roots that envisages the "world as a family" (Vasudhaiva kutumbakam) and 'happiness for all' (Sarve bhavantu sukhinah) have been integrated into policymaking. This has helped him win the faith of the people including the Indian Diaspora. His effective connect with the Diaspora in countries like the USA, UK, Singapore, Australia, and the Gulf has tremendously helped advance India's interests.

Prime Minister Modi's approach to national security is marked by a strong undercurrent of nationalist ideology and a strategic long-term vision of building a strong India. On the security front, the policy of zero tolerance on cross-border terrorism has yielded visible results and ensured a stable India. India's capability and resolve to protect its sovereignty and territorial integrity has enhanced its international credibility. A strong message has been sent that any attempt to change the status quo along the Line of Actual Control will be not only be repulsed but will also receive a befitting response. It is only Prime Minister Modi who has ensured the building of a strategic and strong infrastructure along the borders.

The integration of Jammu and Kashmir with the rest of the country and the creation of two Union Territories of J&K and Ladakh has been the greatest achievement since independence. With government priority on development for the people, the two UTs are witnessing a new era of rapid development. Earlier, terrorism had taken over 41,500 lives between 1989 and 2019. This is evident by the recent initiatives of the Government in empowering grassroots institutions, accelerating development, building infrastructure, reinforcing governance, generating employment, broadening social inclusion, and promoting growth.

Important reforms in the defence sector have been introduced under Prime Minister's vision of Shaktimaan and Atmanirbhar Bharat. The conceptual framework of his clarion call for Aatmanirbhar Bharat brought about a transformational change in the mindset of the entire security community of the nation. Domestic manufacturing has been encouraged. He wants self-reliance to transcend from planning rooms to the battle field. It encompassed all activities from conceptualization, indigenous technology development, design and development capabilities and validation of prototypes to production—all to be executed within the country. The Prime Minister has encouraged harnessing the energies of a larger ecosystem that exists outside the public sector.

Prime Minister Narendra Modi has shown determination of action against efforts in the imposition of unilateral action that may adversely impact India's security interests. However, this has been done in a gradual, calibrated and responsible manner, after exploring every opportunity to resolve disputes through peaceful means. He has also made efforts to upgrade existing structures and build capacities to deal with both contemporary and futuristic security challenges. Most importantly, his initiatives are people-centric and defined by what is good for India and the world at large. With this approach, under his leadership, the country has handled national security challenges, through is a judicious mix of prudence and unflinching resolve.

His approach includes consultation with stake holders, and reliance on experts. This has led to effective strategic planning and speedy decision-making. Prime Minister Modi is willing to break from past precedents, take risks and rise above political considerations in the national interest. Efforts have been made to build a seamless, coordinated national security apparatus and intelligence grid. This has resulted in no major terrorist attack in the recent past. In a world that has witnessed high levels of Islamist terrorism in the past decade, India's effective countering of terrorist threats, despite numerous attempts by extremist groups, is a tribute to his decisive leadership.

The Narendra Modi Government has put great effort into rejuvenating and restoring our cultural heritage across several countries and, thus, reinforcing India's contributions to their legacy. The Modi Government symbolically established Indian ownership of the tradition by working with the United Nations to have 21 June declared as the International Day of Yoga which is now religiously followed every year throughout the world. This has had a lasting impact on India's soft power across the world.

The past two decades have been a period of enormous achievements in politics and policies for Prime Minister Modi. He has worked tirelessly for the people with an inspiring and all-consuming dedication. He has built a stronger and equitable economy. He has helped create a cleaner and transparent polity and administration, not just by personal example but by institutionalizing and future-proofing best practices. He has come to symbolize good, honest and responsive governance.

It is a great honour for India to have assumed the presidency of G-20 under the dynamic leadership of Prime Minister Modi. The leadership of G-20 has come at a very crucial juncture and the world is fortunate to have him as the leader of G-20 at this critical stage, especially to address the burning issues the world faces today.

Prime Minister Modi has always ensured an effective government response in times of calamities. His hands-on style of functioning ensures unwavering commitment and devotion. On numerous occasions in the past two decades, Prime Minister Modi has personally led from the front in rescue operations after calamities struck. Having him at the helm of affairs gave a sense of security to those stranded and waiting to be rescued. Some leaders consciously avoid dealing with crises due to a fear of failing. On the other hand, leaders like Modi step in a crisis and lead from the front in public interest. Through exemplary conduct in situations like natural disasters, infectious disease outbreaks and humanitarian crises, he has demonstrated his deep commitment towards the nation. For Prime Minister Modi, India is always first. He has never shied away from leading from the front and has always demonstrated impeccable leadership. Whenever the public has felt a need, Prime Minister Modi has delivered. This is why he remains the man India trusts in a crisis.

Prime Minister Narendra Modi's commitment to nation-building, an abiding belief in India's inherent potential and a unique leadership style have played important roles in framing strong and effective national security policies. A political leader with a vision of the future and down-to-earth experience of public service and governance, he has three traits that distinguish him from most other leaders—his capacity for hard work, penchant for detail and fast comprehension of complex issues.

Prime Minister Modi recently exhorted fellow Indians to look at the next twenty-five years as 'Amrit Kaal' and highlighted the need for collective effort (Sabka Prayas) to achieve the desired transformation. Several transformative initiatives have been launched to achieve this goal. The Prime Minister's vision has established India's prominence in the world order utilizing new geo-political alignments to suit India's national interests. All these measures and reforms through his proactive policies have made India a leader in all respects, in the region and the world.

2

ADDRESSING INDIA'S SECURITY CONCERNS

General V.K. Singh (Retd.)

India faces a number of security challenges, including terrorism, cyber-attacks, border security, and maritime security. The government, under the leadership of Prime Minister Narendra Modi, has taken a number of steps to address these concerns.

Terrorism: India has faced the threat of terrorism for many years, particularly in the form of cross-border terrorism from Pakistan and extremist violence in some regions of the country.

Prime Minister Modi has taken a strong stance against terrorism and has ordered military strikes against terrorist camps in Pakistan in response to attacks on Indian soil. He has also pushed for international cooperation in the fight against terrorism and has advocated a global crackdown on terrorism financing.

Cyber Security: With the increasing dependence on technology and the rise of cyber threats, Prime Minister Modi has placed a strong emphasis on cyber security. He has launched the Digital India initiative, which aims to make government services easily accessible to citizens through technology and build a secure online infrastructure. The Indian government has also set up a number of agencies and institutions to improve cyber security and respond to cyber threats.

Border Security: India shares land borders with several countries and their security is a key concern for the government. Prime Minister Modi has taken steps to strengthen border security by increasing the presence of security forces and modernizing border management technologies. He has also sought to improve relations with neighbouring countries to reduce the risk of cross-border tensions and conflicts.

Maritime Security: As a coastal country with one of the largest Exclusive Economic Zones (EEZ) in the world, India is also concerned about maritime security. Prime Minister Modi has launched the Sagar Mala project, which aims to modernize India's port infrastructure and develop new ports, thereby enhancing the country's maritime capabilities. The government has also increased the presence of the Indian Navy in the Indian Ocean region to ensure the security of sea lanes of communication.

In conclusion, Prime Minister Modi has taken a number of steps to address India's security concerns, ranging from counterterrorism efforts to improving cyber security and strengthening border and maritime security.

3

Ushering a New Era of Conflict Resolution and Shared Growth: PM Modi's Vision for Mutual & Harmonious Development for All

Meenakshi Lekhi

In the midst of a devastating global pandemic and unprecedented supply chain crisis triggered by both the COVID-induced challenges and the Russia-Ukraine war, which has resulted in many countries suffering from severe balance of payment crisis or have witnessed a massive rise in the price of energy, or are getting sunk into bottomless pits of internal or cross-border conflicts, one of the very few countries that has emerged more resilient through the times of the pandemic and global supply chain crisis, along with robust economic indicators, has been India.

India's Phoenix like Rise through Tumultuous Times

When fears of recession and price rise has been plaguing the whole world, and the immediate estimates of the global economic growth matrix looks bleak, India not only emerged as the fifth-largest economy of the world but is on its track, in spite of several challenges, to become the third-largest economy of the world in the next half decade. Also, having administered more than 220 crores of vaccines, mostly free of cost, to a vast section of its eligible populace and having given free additional rations to more than 80 crore people since the time of the beginning of the COVID pandemic, Prime Minister Modi's pragmatic policies made sure that no eligible Indian was deprived of either vaccines or deserving additional rations. In both ways, he ensured that through the tumultuous times of the pandemic, no Indian had to starve or had to give up the thought of getting vaccinated for lack of financial means. In the absence of either of the two, there would have been social chaos of unprecedented proportions, which was avoided by pragmatic decisions of the Modi government.

Yet it was not just that. Even during the peak of the pandemic, India faced unprecedented challenges along its borders. It was barely a year after Article 370 was abrogated and the threats of a rise in the spate of terror activities in J&K from across the border was always there. Even then, under the deft leadership of Prime Minister Modi, the Government of India not only managed the complex pandemic situation to make sure that India eventually emerged out of it successfully, but also, without giving in to the provocations from across the borders, India did manage well to contain cross-border terrorism in Kashmir to a great extent, and went ahead with developmental work in J&K, and continued with unprecedented border infrastructure development along the northern borders, even as India's armed forces remained operationally deployed for any untoward incident. All these were executed without raising the rhetoric and with profound maturity that eventually made India emerge in a far better situation than many others.

Resolute Actions

It has to be remembered that these measures, even though they seem just acts during times of a pandemic, were crucial to maintain peace and tranquillity and to make sure that India did not plunge into any kind of chaos, even though some within and outside India perhaps did indeed pray for it.

The skilful management of the economy and, taking the nation through complex geopolitical turmoil, made sure that India did not have any food or vaccine crisis. Moreover, the Government of India did not allow any kind of border flare-ups or any major war-like situation to develop. By adequate deployment of forces, India made sure that the message was given loud and clear that while India was all for peace and harmonious collaboration to deal with pandemic-related global challenges, it would certainly not allow any foreign nation to impinge upon India's sovereignty at any cost.

Vaccine Diplomacy

It has to be kept in mind that when many developed countries, especially from the Western hemisphere, were accused of hoarding vaccines, especially during the peak of the COVID pandemic in 2021, India not only demonstrated its industrial scalability by manufacturing hundreds of crores of vaccines, but also made sure that while addressing the needs of its own populace, which is vast by any standard, it also had the heart to give it to 70-odd other countries, especially those who did not have the wherewithal to manufacture it on their own.

Those initiatives by PM Modi went a long way in saving millions of lives across the world. Imagine the chaos that would have erupted had India not taken such benevolent decisions then. Yet, it was not just benevolence but also a visionary act because the world as a whole can certainly not be at peace if scores of underdeveloped or developing countries suffered immeasurably and people continued to die. It would not have served the purpose of global peace, prosperity and harmony if only people of industrialized nations, who could manufacture or purchase vaccines at exorbitant prices, survived.

Aid to Sri Lanka

Not just that, when the people of Sri Lanka were suffering during a severe economy crunch in the island-nation due to a severe balance of payment crisis resulting in appalling shortages of food, medicines and other necessary items, the PM Modi-led Government of India went out of its way to help the people of India's southern neighbour with whom India has cultural, civilizational and religious connect through a shared history since time immemorial.

Altogether, India provided around $ 4 billion in financial assistance and food aid to Sri Lanka that critically helped the country from sinking further into a bottomless pit of internal violence, strife and chaos as a result of economic crisis. For India under Prime Minister Modi, assisting Sri Lanka was not just about benevolence but also about restoring order there because any kind of prolonged internal strife in India's southern neighbourhood would have had potential spill over effect into India as well.

Also, it has to be kept in mind that radical extremist organisations and terror groups wait for such a strife to deepen in countries and then capitalise on such situations to further their own agenda. By bailing out Sri Lanka from that severe economic crisis, India made sure that the poisonous fangs of ISIS-kind organisations did not get a chance to bolster their presence there.

Hope for a Peaceful J&K

Even before the pandemic, the manner in which the PM Modi led Government of India abrogated Article 370 and ushered in a new era of hope for peace in J&K has become for the world to see as a template for conflict resolution. When cynics cried foul that any attempt to dilute or abrogate Article 370 and making J&K an integral part of India, would result in creation of an endless cycle of violence, and potentially even lead to another Indo-Pak conflict, the PM Modi-led Government of India executed a clinical operation to make constitutional amendments to bifurcate J&K and Ladakh, and then declare them as two union territories and put in place an iron grid to make sure that barring sporadic incidents of unrest, no major disturbance, leave alone a war, could be waged by Pakistan.

The constitutional amendments to integrate J&K with the rest of India is now making sure that along with breakneck speed of developmental work, unprecedented commitments of investments are being made by corporate India for J&K. Also, for decades those of J&K who were deprived of social benefits such as reservations in jobs and education, are now being able to avail the same.

It is also to be mentioned that India's cross-border strikes into the heart of Pakistan's terror training bastion in Balakot, in the aftermath of the gruesome Pulwama terror attack, made it amply clear to everyone that India had changed and that it would ferociously strike back if major incidents of terror were to take place ever again. While minor remnants of terrorism still remain in Kashmir and it would take some more time to completely eradicate terrorism; nevertheless, the days of major terror attacks or stone pelting are now entirely over in J&K. Much of this has been accomplished by not just anti-terror operations but also cracking down on hawala routes and narcotics rackets that used to fund stone pelters and anti-India protests in Kashmir.

No Major Terror Attacks: It should also be mentioned that since 2014, when the Prime Minister Modi-led NDA government came to power, India's major cosmopolitan cities have not witnessed any major terror attacks. While part of the reason is the unprecedented anti-terror crack downs that have been executed by India's central agencies against innumerable sleeper cells of cross-border terror groups, the Modi Government also went for the jugular by unleashing severe crackdowns on narcotics being pushed into India from Pakistan. Narcotics smuggling is the prime source of funding for cross-border terror outfits controlled by the deep state of Pakistan.

Likewise, the crackdown on illegal currencies that were being pushed into India also delivered positive results in terms of choking the funds for terror activities. Overall, the expansion of the footprints of the NCB, NIA and sustained intelligence based anti-terror strikes have made sure that Indians in major cities now do not think twice before venturing out to malls and other public places during festive seasons. Compare this with what used to be the scenario before the Modi era started in 2014 when, between 2005 and 2013, serial blasts in major cities of India had almost become a norm rather than an exception. Yet, not much was done by the previous regime to take Pakistan's reign of terror by the horns.

Peace Beckons Northeast

Also, it has to be kept in mind how under the Modi era, the very definition of the northeast part of India is changing from being a region strife with insurgency to emerging as India's gateway to the Far East. Today, Northeast India is brimming with energy and aspiration. Massive infrastructure development, political stability, cross-border strikes by the Indian Army into the heart of secessionist elements and a new wave of connectivity as well as investments, has now brought in unprecedented peace there. Complex challenges including those related to interstate boundary disputes are being solved through dialogue. There is a rising sense of oneness and unity. Needless to say, unlike in the past, states like Assam no more witness bomb blasts or terror attacks. This is the result of Prime Minister Modi's vision of a shared future of harmony and growth.

Hands of Assistance: Over the last few years, the Modi Government has reached out to Nepal, Bangladesh, the Maldives and Sri Lanka and made it clear that India's growth cannot be hers growth alone. Unless they have a shared future with India, India's growth story would be incomplete. From solving long-pending boundary issues with Bangladesh to pouring in Indian investments to neighbouring states, India under PM Modi has striven to take everyone along. Even during critical crises in distant parts of the world, India took the initiative to airlift her own people back, be it from Yemen or Ukraine. It took the initiative to bring back people from her neighbourhood as well.

G20 Presidency: As India takes over the presidency of G20 for 2023, increasingly, the world, and especially the countries of the global South, are looking up to India to usher in a new era of peace and tranquillity in the world. The iconic phrase of *Vasudhaiva Kutumbakam* has been made the theme of G20 for the year 2023 in India. Through this, PM Modi's message is loud and clear that it is time for the whole world to be looked at as one family with one future. It is important to look at all people as members of one family. Unless that is done and so long the world is a perceived prism of differences and concepts of 'Us' versus 'Them', conflicts will not end. For more than eight years now, through various actions, the Modi Government has shown that India's conflict-resolution mechanisms and bold steps to manage complex crises even while taking care of the downtrodden, can be a template for the world. Through actions, India is increasingly telling the world that this century can genuinely become a century of peace and not of war. And India has a template to offer to the rest of the world. This template of universal peace comes from a country which is at the same time a responsible nuclear power, an economic powerhouse, an emerging industrial giant, and yet one who does not forget to empathise with the downtrodden and dares to speak for the voiceless. That is the true essence of the genuine peacemaker that India has been for eternity.

4

Security under the Narendra Modi Government

Dr. Bibek Debroy

The word 'security' has many dimensions. Etymologically, it means to be free from anxiety. Therefore, there are elements of national security and economic security, at the level of the aggregate and, in parallel, at the level of the individual or household. Across various dimensions, every once in a while, someone tries to quantify security through an index. An example of this is the World Happiness Report and in the 2022 version, India ranks 136th, behind Pakistan at 121st and Sri Lanka at 127th.[1] (Bangladesh is 94th.) It would be hard to argue that a resident of Pakistan or Sri Lanka is more secure today than an Indian resident. For that matter, one wonders what a British resident (ranked 17th) would say. However, that's neither here nor there, and exhibits folly of such cross-country rankings and comparisons, rather than anything else.

The COVID pandemic caught India, like the rest of the world, unawares. It was an exogenous shock. Indeed, most recent shocks have been imposed by developed countries on emerging market economies. At that time, it was the prevalent wisdom from the developed world that India would go under. Millions would die. By any metric, when normalized for population, India has performed remarkably well. Both infection rates and mortality rates have been low. At that time, it was the prevalent wisdom that India would never be able to develop a vaccine of its own and, regardless, would not be able to vaccinate its population. Both propositions have been proved to be false. India has handled this externally-imposed disaster remarkably well, facilitated by the emphasis on a digital India and portability of welfare benefits.[2] Under the Epidemic Diseases Act of 1897, there was little the Union Government could do, beyond action taken at the border. Success in controlling the pandemic involved cooperation with the states.

In debates on fiscal policy, at that time, it was the recommended doctrine that, emerging from the lockdown and pandemic, India should increase public expenditure, meaning revenue expenditure, to stimulate the economy. With the exception of free food (Pradhan Mantri Garib Kalyan Anna Yojana), nothing of the sort was done. The Union Government increased capital expenditure, recognizing that the multiplier effects of capital expenditure are more than twice that on revenue expenditure, and did not throw fiscal caution to the winds. Therefore, so far as the macroeconomic fundamentals are concerned, India is one of the fastest-growing economies in the world, this financial year, and also in the foreseeable future. Even on inflation, caused primarily by imported inflation, India has done remarkably well.

Economic security is influenced by the macro environment. The macro environment, first because of the pandemic and second because of geo-political tensions centred around USA-Ukraine, has turned inimical. In the midst of this, the Modi government has provided an environment that reduces uncertainty and provides economic security. There are several dimensions to this, several of which are a continuation of policies pursued since May 2014. First, there has been an enabling framework for growth, development and entrepreneurship to blossom and flourish. There are elements of ease of doing business in this and elements of ease of living. Second, there has been inclusion, interpreted as empowerment. A part of this is through provision of collective private goods—transport, education, health, electricity, gas, toilets, water, technology and financial products. This enables historically deprived and marginalized sections of society to become mainstreamed. The *Economic Survey 2020-21* constructed a "bare necessities" index (BNI) to quantify and measure these improvements. The remaining part was use of SECC to target subsidies to eligible beneficiaries, with DBT (direct benefit transfers) linked to bank accounts seeded with Aadhaar numbers. Other than government dashboards, these improvements were evident in third-party audits and in responses to questions in the National Family Health Survey (NFHS-5). Thus, it is no great surprise that UNDP's 2022 report, using the multi-dimensional poverty index (MDPI), found that a large number of Indians had been raised above the poverty line.

Third, when the pandemic broke, these initiatives worked to India's advantage. Other than vaccination, as a consequence of providing social security, the vulnerable population was cushioned from the effects of both COVID and the lockdown. In addition, portability of social welfare benefits, additional supply of free food and registration of unorganized sector labour kicked in. Hence, because of supply-side measures, recovery from the lockdown was swift. This financial year, in 2022-23, real growth is expected to be of the order of 7 per cent, give or take a decimal point. The figure is projected to be around 6.5 per cent in the medium term. This makes India one of the fastest growing economies in the world. Nor has inflation, one of the successes of the Modi government since May 2014, spun out of control. Nor have deficits increased inordinately. Fourth, to belabour the point further, the four sources of growth are net exports, consumption, private investments and government expenditure. Many countries in the world have suffered because of their excessive dependence on exports alone. In contrast, India possesses those three other engines of growth too. As was mentioned, the Union Government expenditure has concentrated on capital expenditure and the government has progressively liberalized and eased regulations to facilitate entry of private investments. Thus, if security is interpreted in the economic sense, in the sense of ease of living and ease of doing business, there is a lot the Narendra Modi government has done since May 2014, to improve India's growth potential and productivity.

Moving beyond economic security, internal security has dimensions of terrorism, left-wing extremism (LWE), insurgency in the North-east and cross-border terrorism in Jammu & Kashmir. As details given in the annual report of the Ministry of Home Affairs documents, all of these have declined in importance, also evident from journalistic reports and anecdotal impressions.[3] To take one example, in 2014, the number of LWE incidents was 1,091 and the number of deaths was 310. In 2020, the respective figures were 665 and 183 and one can clearly see the pattern of a decline in numbers over time. "The geographical spread of LWE violence has also been shrinking considerably. In 2020, LWE violence was reported from 226 PSs in 53 districts spread across nine states as compared to 328 PSs in 76 districts spread over 10 states in 2013. The arc of violence has been considerably restricted with just 30 districts accounting for88 per cent of the LWE violence."[4] This is replicated in the case of the North-east. "The security situation in the NE states has improved substantially since 2014. The year 2020 recorded the lowest insurgency incidents and casualties among civilians and security forces during the last two decades. Compared to 2014, there has been an 80 per cent reduction in insurgency incidents in 2020. Similarly, in this period, SFs casualties have come down by 75 per cent and civilian deaths by 99 per cent."[5] The pattern is no different for cross-border incidents. There is an inevitable problem in perceptions about security. A security lapse, leading to some kind of incident, attracts a lot of attention. However, tightened and heightened security, preventing an incident, remains relatively invisible. Indeed, the primary role of this kind of security is preventive and the fact that there has been no major incident since 2014 is testimony to the success. In this connection, one should also mention cooperation with other countries in matters connected with international terrorism, organized crime and illicit trafficking in narcotic drugs.

Security is about the present. It is also about the future. India is now in the midst of Amrit Kaal, setting out the template for the next twenty-five years. However interpreted, is India more secure in 2022 than in 2014, notwithstanding the external shocks that have been thrust upon us? The answer is undoubtedly in the affirmative. Is there a vision in place, to make India more secure in 2047 than in 2022? The answer to that too is in the affirmative. That more or less sums up the success of the Narendra Modi government in providing security.

Endnotes

1. https://worldhappiness.report/ed/2022/happiness-benevolence-and-trust-during-covid-19-and-beyond/#ranking-of-happiness-2019-2021
2. See, for instance, the essay, "A New Epoch Begins," in N.K. Singh and P.K. Mishra, *Recalibrate, Changing Paradigms*, Rupa, 2022.
3. *Annual Report 2020-21*, Ministry of Home Affairs, https://www.mha.gov.in/sites/default/files/MHAARE_22042022.pdf
4. Ibid.
5. Ibid.

5

Minimum Government, Maximum Governance 2014–Present: Purposeful Policy Making in India

Amitabh Kant

Almost five years ago, Prime Minister Narendra Modi had challenged the bureaucracy to transform the lives of citizens in the 112 most backward districts of India. He did not term them as "backward" but called them the "Aspirational Districts" of India. These districts included some of the most far-flung, complex and difficult districts and were selected through a transparent process. Over the last four years, these districts have seen transformative changes across health and nutrition, education, financial inclusion and basic infrastructure because of the convergence of all government programmes and real-time monitoring and ranking of districts on 49 different indicators. This flow of data on a real-time basis, use of technology, challenging districts and States on good governance through ranking and building tech platforms has been the hallmark of reforms and restructuring of governance in India during the last eight years. This technological leapfrogging of governance is driving efficiency and effectiveness and will yield rich dividends in productivity on a sustained basis.

Years ago, I was working in the traditional fisheries sector of Kerala. My job was to enhance the returns of fishermen who were getting a mere 20 per cent of the market price of fish. The biggest challenge was to open bank accounts for fishermen. The process of "Know Your Customer" was a nightmare. It took us ten months of chasing physical banks and bank managers to do this. Contrast this with the experience today. You can walk into a bank branch and open a bank account using biometric authentication in one minute flat. From ten months to one minute has been the stunning paradigm shift. According to the global index report released by the World Bank, a whopping 55 per cent of all bank accounts created across the world during 2014-17 were opened in India. Of the 470 million PMJDY bank accounts opened till date, around 55 per cent are held by women. The vast coverage of Jan Dhan accounts has also provided a key impetus to India's extensive adoption of digital payment modes such as the UPI and debit cards, with 31 crore RuPay cards now been issued. This is almost 30 per cent of the total number of debit and credit cards in circulation, with the number crossing one billion recently.

Let us look at the scale of technological transformation in the last few years. The government put its energy in getting the JAM (Jan-Dhan Aadhaar Mobile) trinity going. This forms the basic data infrastructure for India's stack consisting of e-KYC, e-Sign, instantaneous payments (Unified Payments Interface) and digilockers. This has been the single biggest factor for the expansion of financial inclusion in India and has presented a unique model for the world. For people to get subsidies or social benefits, they needed a bank account. Hence, under PMJDY, a no-frills bank account for all Indian adults was opened, all of them linked with Aadhaar. When I was a young officer, our then Prime Minister had said that out of every rupee transferred to the poor, there is a leakage of 85 paise. In sharp contrast, today India undertakes a cumulative direct benefit transfer of almost 26 lakh crore. In 426 operational schemes across 56 ministries, there is not a single paise of leakage. Direct benefit transfer and governance reforms have increased the government's efficiency to target beneficiaries directly. This has enabled India to remove duplicate and fake beneficiaries and plug leakages. During the pandemic, this robust network of direct benefit transfers enabled the provision of immediate relief to millions. The next key transformation has been in the sphere of digital payments. India had hitherto been entirely a cash economy.

Thanks to BHIM/UPI, consumer bill payments have become extremely simple and easy. We have seen the emergence of UPI-based transaction platforms such as Google Pay, Samsung Pay, PhonePe, and Paytm. India clocked 730 crore transactions in October 2022 worth INR 12.11 lakh crore, the highest ever. India's approach to digital platforms has been unique. We are creating platforms where government creates the brick and mortar of the foundational layer with start-ups and innovative enterprises building interfaces and layers on top. The effort has been to break silos through real-time governance and move away from a case-to-case approach to systematic governance with meaningful participation of stakeholders. These are all next-gen reforms.

A great example of this is the government e-Marketplace (GeM) which is the national public procurement portal, all online end-to-end for open, efficient and transparent procurement of goods and services by the government. The platform has transformed legacy procurement systems through a disruptive marketplace model and the use of technology, analytics and digitization of process. It is an example of minimum government and maximum governance. Similarly, the National Agriculture Market (eNAM) is an electronic trading portal which networks the existing mandis under the agriculture product market committees to create a unified national market for agricultural commodities. It removes information asymmetry between buyers and sellers and promotes real-time price discovery based on structural demand and supply.

I recall that in the first presentation that I made to Prime Minister Modi in June 2014 as the then Secretary, DIPP, I was directed to focus on Ease of Doing Business and make India easy and simple. India was then ranked 142 in the World Bank's EODB Index and in the previous four years had only worsened its position. Since then, a vast number of rules, regulations, processes and over 1,400 laws have been eliminated. As a consequence, India has jumped up 79 positions in the global rankings—the only large country in the world to have made such a quantum jump. Our target is to get into the top 50 next year and within the top 25 in the next three years. In a federal country like India, it is the states that attract investments. We, therefore, started ranking states on outcomes. There was an intense competition. The first year, Gujarat came number one. The very next year, Andhra Pradesh beat Gujarat and in the third year, Telangana and Andhra emerged on top. However, the good thing was that eastern states like Jharkhand and Chhattisgarh made radical reforms and came fourth and fifth. My belief is that if competition can transform eastern states, highly resource-rich India will have long-term equitable growth.

Accompanying this was reforming the entire Foreign Direct Investment regime. We piloted different proposals for liberalizing sector after sector and abolish the Foreign Investment Promotion Board. All of them were approved by the Prime Minister. These reforms have led FDI inflows in India growing and expanding from US$ 36 billion in 2013-14 to US$ 83 billion in 2022. This, despite the global FDI flows falling sharply during the same period. We are on track to achieve $ 100 billion FDI.

From exporting zero mobile phones in 2014, today we have become a mobile phone exporting country worth thousands of crores. Today, in India, a person is using an average of 14 GB data on mobiles in a month. In 2014, the cost of this 14 GB data was around Rs. 4,200 per month. Today, the same amount of data is available for Rs. 100 or Rs. 150. In the last eight years, our poverty rate has reduced from 22 per cent to 10 per cent, and extreme poverty fell below 1 per cent and remained static at 0.8 per cent. Our per capita income doubled while foreign reserves also increased two-fold. India created the second largest road network in the world, and our solar and wind power generation capacity doubled in the past five years. In 2012-13, our food grain production was 255 million tonnes, which increased to 316.06 million tonnes in 2021-22, the highest ever in our history. Despite the global economic slowdown due to the COVID-19 pandemic, India managed to clock a record in merchandise exports at $ 418 billion in the last financial year.

Next, realizing that entrepreneurship technology and innovation are at the heart of transforming India, the Government launched the Start-up India movement. An increasing number of advanced technology start-ups, the rising adoption of data analytics, artificial intelligence and internet of things in everyday processes and continuing investor interest in Indian start-ups have created a dynamic ecosystem. Many of India's start-ups are revolutionizing service delivery and quality across several emerging areas of growth. A large number of them are finding solutions for the unique challenges of India and several of them are leveraging technology to enhance health and education outcomes. In a very short while, we have developed the second-best ecosystem for start-ups in the world with 107 unicorns. To encourage innovation re-engineering of proceedings, online filing of patents and trademarks was undertaken. This led to patent examination increasing from 22,631 in 2014-15 to 800,088 by 2019-20. The time required for patent examination has reduced from six years to a mere 12 months. The period of examination of new trademarks has reduced from 13 months to less than 30 days.

Some commentators have argued that this is a government which believes in gradualism and has not undertaken big-ticket reforms. Some others have spoken about implementation on the ground. Nothing can be farther from the truth. Two of the biggest reforms ushered are the Goods and Services Tax and the Bankruptcy Code. Creating the GST council, a new federal arrangement where the Centre has only a 33 per cent vote and states account for 66 per cent with any dispute requiring a 75 per cent support has been path breaking. It subsumed 17 taxes and multiple cesses, aligning India with global regimes, ended long queues of trucks at state borders and created a seamless national market. The Insolvency and Bankruptcy Code has been a key economic reform leading to faster recovery of stressed assets and quicker resolution. It has instilled a better sense of credit discipline and for the first time in India, there is seriousness among defaulting borrowers because of the fear of losing their assets on the ground in a time-bound manner if the resolution process fails. A vast number of cases are being disposed of even prior to the IBC process as the borrowers make good amounts in default to the creditors. Another tough bullet to bite has been the Real Estate Regulation Act (RERA) which has brought discipline in the construction sector, provided protection to consumers and ensured that delivery of ongoing construction is a seamless process.

The Ujjwala Yojana (providing 8 crore cooking gas connections to below poverty line families), Ujala (distribution of 123 million LED bulbs saving 43 million kilowatts hour per day) and Deen Dayal Upadhyaya Gram Jyoti

Yojana (providing electrification to even the remotest Indian villages) are examples of speedy time bound implementation on the ground. In India, the case study of the UJALA (Unnat Jyoti by Affordable LEDs for All) scheme is a phenomenal example of how a sustainable lifestyle habit shift substantially reduced India's carbon footprint. A few years ago, the government launched a campaign to encourage the use of LED bulbs. The campaign had a three-pronged agenda—to reduce electricity bills for consumers, bring down costs of electricity and also protect the environment. Till date, the scheme has saved close to 48 million kwh of energy per year since its launch. It has also led to cost savings of approximately INR 19,000 crore. Within a short time, more than 160 crore LED bulbs were installed in Indian homes. Consequently, UJALA resulted in a reduction of more than 100 million tonnes of carbon dioxide emissions.

The redefinition of the MSME sector based on turnover which was held up for over two decades, the commercial mining of coal, the massive liberalization of the mineral sector and the announcement that the public sector would remain only in a few strategic sectors clearly demonstrate the determination of the government to make structural reforms. These are all path-breaking measures. There is a clear intent that business must be driven to size, scale and efficiency by the private sector and the government must only be a catalyst.

The government has also sent out a clear message to investors across the world by restructuring its direct tax regime. It slashed the corporate tax structure to 15 per cent for new manufacturing companies and 22 per cent for all companies. The new rates bring India on par with most OECD and neighbouring countries like China and Indonesia. The lower rates will reduce the cost of capital and catalyse investments. According to a Morgan Stanley report, the nation is expected to drive nearly 20 per cent of the world's growth in the coming decade, more than doubling its own GDP—from $ 3.5 trillion today to over $ 7.5 trillion by 2031. In the next five years, India is also forecasted to surpass Japan and Germany to become the world's third-largest economy and stock market, signalling a "once-in-a-generation shift" of its economic position.

In my view, the best examples of the reformist zeal of the government was demonstrated by two key social programmes—the Swachh Bharat Mission and Ayushman Bharat. Both have gone beyond being mere government schemes and have become the shared vision of the entire nation. I have admired SBM as it did not lay emphasis on the construction of toilets but focused on behavioural change and outcomes. It succeeded because of a strong political will and the PM's personal commitment and the fact that it was demand-driven. Out-of-pocket healthcare expenses which are catastrophic push nearly 66 lakh households of India into poverty every year. Ayushman Bharat, through 150,000 health and wellness centres, is shifting the focus of healthcare provision towards providing primary healthcare to its citizens. PMJAY, while providing insurance to 50 crore beneficiaries, will leverage facilities in public and private hospitals and is one of the largest public-funded health insurance schemes in the world. It has been a remarkable success story.

Launched by Prime Minister Narendra Modi in January 2018, the Aspirational Districts Programme (ADP) seeks to improve socio-economic outcomes by reimagining governance, vesting greater ownership and accountability in the district administration, facilitating convergence and collaboration among stakeholders, tracking performance indicators on a real-time basis as well as engaging citizens to contribute to the development process. Since its launch, all 112 underdeveloped districts included in the programme have significantly improved their performance. While some have surpassed the state averages on key indicators, many Aspirational Districts are now the best performing of all districts in their state. The Prime Minister changed the development narrative by referring to backward districts as 'aspirational' instead of 'backward'. By doing so, he ensured that no district in the country was left behind in the journey towards development for all. Given India's size and diversity, it is crucial that states and districts have a greater say in their own development. This is the crux of competitive federalism. Moreover, local challenges differ significantly across the country. State and local governments are therefore best positioned to recognise their development challenges, and design customised policy interventions. This move is grounded in evidence which shows that devolution of resources and responsibilities to lower levels of government can lead to better governance of facilities in the public sector, higher use of public services and greater achievement of desired socio-economic outcomes.

The last eight years have seen wide-ranging reforms and there are several implementation success stories that have transformed the lives of the citizens at grassroots levels. The 1991 reforms were essentially industrial delicensing reforms. Recent reforms cut across technology, innovation, institutions, FDI, governance and, most importantly, social welfare have transformed several unreformed key sectors and significantly improved the quality of life of Indian citizens. Together, they represent a watershed reform moment which will drive India's growth and prosperity.

6

Economic Reforms Since 2014

Rajiv Mehrishi

The well-intentioned, though misguided, Fabian socialism of India's first prime minister, and the largely cynical socialism of his successors, shattered India's hopes, so evocatively expressed by Pandit Nehru himself, of keeping its tryst with destiny. The Congress Party's nationalisation and regulatory urge gained momentum when it needed the support of leftist parties to remain in power. The first phase of bank nationalisation came in 1969 with the avowed aim of "alleviating poverty". The party perhaps ascribed, to a significant extent, its landslide victory in the 1971 elections to such Garibi Hatao slogans. Hence, we continued on this destructive path, nationalising almost every wealth and job-creating sector: coal, steel, copper, oil companies, refining, cotton textiles and insurance. Industries that were not nationalised were put under strict regulatory control that spawned the infamous "licence raj". The error was compounded with the stress on heavy industries, "start(ing) from the heavy, basic, mother industries to the production of iron and steel on a large scale. We must start with the production of the machine that make machines" (Nehru, 1956). The consequence was that the limited capital available in the country got sequestered by large industry, almost wholly in public sector organisations.

The ill effects of these economically suicidal policies were felt in every sphere, including education and health; in fact, the low rates of economic growth (derisively called the "Hindu rate of growth" by the socialist economists themselves) defeated the avowed purpose of these socialist policies—removal, or at least the reduction, of poverty. The decade of reforms, under the able leadership of Narsimha Rao and Vajpayee did much to start the work of bringing down this edifice, so surreal that it sometimes seemed like a conspiracy to keep India and Indians poor. The resultant reduction in the number of poor has been incontrovertibly brought out by Jagdish Bhagwati and Arvind Pangariya in their book *Why Growth Matters*.

However, much work remained, and remains, to be done. However, the "Indian Socialist Network", led by long-time members of the largely English-speaking members of the Lutyens Club was, and remains, a serious stumbling block. What followed, therefore, was a decade (2004-2014) that "locusts hath eaten". In 2014, the Modi government came to power on the promises, made both explicitly and implicitly of addressing the challenge of making a break with the past, of letting free the ingenious people of India to pursue the path of growth and economic prosperity that would finally end poverty in the country. At the end of eight years, it is obvious that the Modi government has carried out some vital and far-reaching reforms. It is equally true that vested interests continue to obstruct some well-meaning reforms. Some of the reforms that have been carried out are discussed in subsequent paragraphs.

One significant, though less talked about and discussed, reform was the introduction, by law, of inflation targeting in the Monetary Policy. Monetary Policy, which is largely the setting of the rate of interest at which the RBI will loan money to the banks (the so-called Repo Rate) is determined by the Reserve Bank of India. In 2015-16, first through an agreement and then by law, the government made it incumbent on the RBI to target that inflation in the country be 4 per cent with a tolerance limit of plus/minus 2 per cent. In other words, inflation is now targeted to be not below 2 per cent and not above 6 per cent. Moreover, the setting of the monetary policy was no longer left to the whims of the RBI Governor but was henceforth to be finalized by a Monetary Policy Committee of six persons, three of whom would be external experts. The reform has served India well. Inflation since 2015-16 has been under control and when, due to the global impact of the economic sanctions imposed on Russia because of the Russia-Ukraine war it did remain beyond 6 per cent for three quarters, RBI was required to explain to the government in writing why inflation had been higher than the tolerance limit and what steps did the RBI intend to take to bring it under control, and by what time did it expect to be able to do so.

The reform has not been discussed widely perhaps because it is not so well understood. However, compulsory inflation targeting is not some esoteric economic concept that can only be understood by so called intellectuals. As is obvious, inflation impacts every citizen of this country. The poor are hit the hardest by high rates of inflation as their income/wages simply cannot keep pace with rising costs, and even the most essential items such as food grains start becoming beyond the reach of the poorest. An inflationary economy is also not conducive to investments and adversely impacts exports. Jobs too, therefore, tend to shrink. Therefore, it is clear that inflation targeting will help the low-income groups as much, if not more, than their richer counterparts. It is surprising that this pro-poor reform has got so little attention in the media or even amongst the average politicians.

Another landmark reform for which the government has not got the credit that it deserves is the enactment of the Indian Bankruptcy Code. Among the leading economies of the world, India was unique in not having a proper bankruptcy law. This gave unscrupulous investors/industrialists an easy way to enrich themselves. They would take huge loans from nationalised banks, find clever ways of sucking out the capital from the industry, sequestering it for themselves and their uber-rich lifestyles. The industry consequently became sick, and the banks could do precious little about it except to file proceedings in the socialist-era toothless organisation, the Bureau of Industrial and Financial Reconstruction (BIFR); after 1993, proceedings under the Recovery of Debts and Bankruptcy Act, 1993; and when this too remained ineffectual to file proceedings under the equally lengthy and frustrating process under the Securitisation and Reconstruction of Financial Assets and Enforcement of Security Interest Act, 2002 (SARFAESI Act) 2002. The non-existence of an effective bankruptcy law is what gave rise to the uniquely Indian phenomena of there being sick industries but no sick industrialists. Plainly put, a small group of people were scamming huge amounts of money from the banking system. Of course, there were a large number of cases of genuine failure of business, which is bound to happen in any free market economy, providing a competitive playfield to all the actors. In either case, whether it be a straightforward scam or a genuine business failure, the outcome (in the absence of an effective bankruptcy law) was that precious and limited capital of the country remained locked, and was not available for deployment in more productive investment which would have generated jobs both directly and indirectly. Unresolved bankruptcies are thus bad news both for the GDP and the job market.

The Insolvency and Bankruptcy Code 2016 (IBC) has changed the landscape entirely. Major cases of loan defaults (NPAs) have been resolved in double quick time: names such as Bhushan Steel, Essar Steel, Amptek Auto, Binani Cement, Ruchi Soya, etc., come to mind. If a sick industry has been bought over by a more successful company, then the sick company would be nursed back to health producing not only goods but also retaining, even increasing, jobs. Equally, whatever discounted money was paid for the sick industry would now be free to be deployed in more productive successful enterprises, again adding to the GDP and the number of jobs in the country. Where resolutions have not been possible and liquidation has become necessary (which happens half the time) precious capital would be released by sale of assets including the precious land assets, again making capital available for investment in more successful and productive enterprises. The IBC is a success story through and through and it is surprising that this important reform was not put in place for seventy years after independence. PM Modi has displayed genuine economic sagacity in having this law enacted.

Another watershed reform has been in the field of indirect taxation. The introduction and successful implementation of the Goods and Services Tax (GST) is of immense benefit to both consumers and businesses, neither of which have now to pay sales tax/VAT on the indirect taxes already imposed in the course of imports or imposed by the state in which the goods were manufactured. Tax at each stage is now paid only on value addition, thus effectively bringing down cost of raw material and finished goods. Without doubt this would also contribute to making our exports more competitive.

The introduction of GST has obviously reduced both the incentive and scope for tax evasion. Since GST has to be paid only on value add, suppliers/manufacturers/retailers have lower tax liabilities and, therefore, perhaps do not find it worth the risk or cost of evading tax. On the other hand, since at each stage the raw material supplier/manufacturer/wholesaler/retailer would like to claim input tax credit to remain competitive and therefore, would not accept inputs/goods on which tax has not been paid. The result is there for all to see: ever increasing GST revenues which have now crossed Rs. 1.5 lakh crore a month.

What makes GST really attractive is that the increase in tax revenues comes even as prices for consumers are lower, and the economy as a whole becomes more efficient, especially with there being no variation in the law or rates of taxation across India's 28 states and 9 Union Territories.

Some critics have pointed out that GST has had an adverse impact on some small scale and medium industries, and that many of such businesses have had to close down. It is difficult to verify if this is actually so, especially as the number of workers enrolled with EPF has steadily increased. Moreover, even if this is true, the extent of the alleged problem is not really known. However, logically speaking if some small and medium scale industry had been adversely affected by GST to the extent of closure, then obviously their economic viability depended largely, if not entirely, on tax evasion. It is a moot question if such enterprises should continue to exist. (It needs to be mentioned that if evasion of indirect taxes is lower, then evasion of direct taxes becomes that much harder too).

The current government's strong belief in and initiatives towards digitalisation have also brought immense benefits to both the economy and in service delivery. In the field of finance, increased digitalisation means more formalisation of the economy, less evasion of taxes and less use/generation of black money. India is reported to have had 70 billion financial transactions digitally in the year 2022. In value terms, India is reportedly averaging digital financial transactions worth Rs. 20,000 crore per day.

Digitisation has had significant advantages. It has allowed Direct Benefit Transfers (DBT), eliminating middlemen and, therefore, reaching the benefit to the targeted beneficiary. No discussion on digitisation is complete without the unbelievably successful vaccination against COVID program. Through the Co-WIN and Arogya Sethu platforms 220 crore vaccination doses have been enabled, meaning that most Indian adults are fully vaccinated. It takes only three simple steps on the Co-WIN platform to get an appointment for vaccination. Though India has delivered the largest number of doses in the world, several times more than any developed country, there is hardly been any complaint about the appointment process or the administering of the vaccine. While full credit needs to go to our doctors and paramedics in actually administering the vaccination, the fact that it was done in such an orderly fashion was only because of the digital platform being provided as a public good. The appointment process also enabled proper planning of supplies of both vaccines and syringes as well as issuance of vaccination certificates digitally—something that even the USA was unable to do.

Privatisation

What defines a communist, or even a socialist, state is control. The state wants to control every aspect of not only an individual's life, but also all economic activity. A necessary consequence is the proliferation of mostly loss-making, inefficient and corrupt public sector undertakings in almost every sphere of economic activity—whether in manufacturing or in the services sector. In spite of India never being reduced to total communism of the Lenin-Stalin or Mao style, the Indian Government blundered into almost all sectors—banking, insurance, road transport, airlines, steel, telecommunication, hotels, manufacture of watches, TVs, tractors and even textiles.

It may seem trite to say that it is not the government's business to do business. Yet, the Indian State blundered, often thoughtlessly, into every business. Not surprisingly, most of these enterprises made losses within years of their starting. In fact, unless the government also ensured monopoly (such as for oil companies) the PSUs almost always made losses of varying degrees, and provided goods or services well below acceptable levels. Some PSUs could not make profits even in monopoly situations—Air India, State Electricity Boards, and most Road Transport Corporations being prime examples. There were several reasons for this loss-making habit but, inevitably, they were almost always rooted in the fact of government ownership.

Apart from being bad economics, these investments seem to also raise an ethical and moral issue. The money that the government invested in these PSUs—first to create them, and then to sustain them, often to the extent of even paying salaries—belonged to the people of a rather poor country. In every sense, the poor in India sacrificed a substantial portion of their scarce wealth into creating and sustaining these loss-making or at least grossly inefficient PSUs. Do not the citizens of this country have a right to demand a return on their equity, and a return of their loans to PSUs, with interest? As a citizen, is it not my wealth that the Government has squandered for meeting its political ends and/or the power of control and the benefits that it brings to those in powerful positions?

The government of Shri Vajpayee took commendable steps to right this historical wrong. Though slow and careful to begin with, the present government now seems to be moving in the right direction. The seemingly impossible task of privatising Air India has been accomplished. The government has also taken the courageous and extremely necessary step of addressing the other elephants in the room: to begin the process of privatising public sector banks whose singular achievement seems to have been to run up huge NPAs. It is now proposed to amend the Bank Nationalisation Act. If anything, the government needs to do yet more. For example, there is no earthly reason why the government should be running hotels, airports, or why the monopoly of the railways should continue in providing services.

Privatisation should not be restricted only to privatising government businesses. It should also mean allowing the private sector to enter and compete in areas where public sector presence may continue. The government has taken significant steps towards this too. For example, defence production has been opened to the private sector, as it should have been decades back. It was hypocritical of us to not allow the private sector in India to produce defence-related equipment (the sector was reserved for the public sector), and yet buy expensive arms and equipment from private manufacturers in Britain, France and the USA. The Modi government has, in fact, exceeded all expectations by allowing the private sector to participate in and contribute to the space sector. When one thinks of it logically there is no justification for ISEO's monopoly to continue, especially as it may make it difficult for us to access latest and innovative technologies in this critical sector of the future.

From the country's point of view, one of the most critical reforms carried out by the Modi government has been replacing the politics of "*revdis*" (handing out freebies with the sole intention of winning elections) with the politics of investment for economic growth. The most gladdening aspect of this is the stress that has been laid on the improvement of infrastructure, especially the road, rail and port infrastructure. India is now making 40 km of national highways each day and the Road Transport Minister aspires to take it to 60 km a day. Equally importantly, the government has shifted gear to making world-class and state-of-the-art highways. The about to be opened Delhi-Mumbai highway which will reduce travel time to Mumbai from 24 to 12 hours is a case in point. Similarly, the cargo handling capacity of Indian ports has almost doubled: increasing from 872 million tonnes per annum in FY 2014-15 to 1,600 million tonnes in FY 2021-22. In railways, the increase in capital expenditure has been even more breathtaking. In 2014-15 capex in the railways was Rs. 46,000 crore; in 2021-22 it was 2,15,000 crore. These high levels of capital investment should help the railways increase its share of freight movement from around 27 per cent to up to 45 per cent. This will not only reduce both congestion on Indian roads and pollution from vehicular emissions but will also make Indian goods more competitive as railways remain by far the cheapest mode of transporting goods in India. For passengers too, services are improving with the introduction of fast trains such as Vande Bharat and the soon-to-be-started Bullet Train from Mumbai to Ahmedabad, which is likely to set in motion a series of similar projects based on similar or improved technology.

The above are a few examples of the important economic reforms undertaken by the Modi government. This is by no means an exhaustive list. But for the constraints of space, many more of these reforms could have been discussed. The reduction in corruption as a result of measures such as faceless tax assessment; the enactment of the Real Estate Regulatory Act in spite of strong opposition by builders' groups, which has gone a long way in protecting the lifelong savings of the middleclass when they invest their savings to buy a home of their home; the government's commitment to reduce pollution as embodied in the LIFE program; the attempt to eliminate exemptions in Income Tax laws by offering a lower Corporate Tax of 25 per cent; a similar lower tax rate for start-ups; the successful implementation of the Swach Bharat program and making India ODF, which will not only make the population more productive but will also reduce the spend, both public and personal, on curative health care; and so on. Unfortunately, some progressive reforms have had to be reversed because of vested interests creating an atmosphere of distrust. The progressive farm laws are a case in point.

On the whole, however, the record of the Modi government in carrying out economic reforms in the last eight years has been impressive.

7

India as a Responsible Global Power

Sujan Chinoy

Recently, at an event organised by the Permanent Mission of India to the United Nations in New York, UN Deputy Secretary General Amina Mohammed summarised a global sentiment when she hailed India for its 'thoughtful leadership and commitment' to advancing high-impact South-South cooperation.[1] The fact is that India under the leadership of Prime Minister Narendra Modi has never let geography or geometry "define us" as it assists countries across the developing world. The event marking the fifth anniversary of the $150 million India-UN Development Fund took place at a time when, as Amina Mohammed put it, the Covid-19 pandemic had demonstrated in stark terms the need for global, intergenerational solidarity and new ways to cooperate towards the achievement of the 2030 Agenda.

Appreciation for India's initiatives over the last eight years of the Modi era is a recognition of the fact that India "walks the talk" when it comes to playing a responsible role in dealing with issues of social and economic development, healthcare and technological advancement particularly in the developing world. Even at the height of the Covid-19 pandemic, India provided 250 million vaccine doses to 101 countries, apart from other medical assistance.

Recently Mexican President Andres Manuel Lopez Obrador proposed that the UN set up a commission comprising PM Narendra Modi, Pope Francis and UN Secretary General Antonio Guterres to establish a five-year truce.[2] He called for the three of them to get together and present a proposal to "stop the war everywhere". That the Mexican President thought of Prime Minister Modi as the only Head of State/Government fit to be on such a proposed world peace commission speaks volumes for India's credibility at this juncture as a nation wedded to the principle of peaceful solutions to the most vexatious of conflicts, even as the Russia-Ukraine war rages in Europe with no sign that either Russia or Ukraine and its supporters such as the US and the EU, are willing to consider a solution other than through war and bloodshed.

Transition in Past Eight Years

Over the last eight years, India has launched new efforts to advance its transition from a state of indecision to a New India, supported by the spirit of change. As a result, the country is fundamentally reshaping its global engagements and deepening domestic reforms to become a global power. Acting on the firm belief that the time has come for India to play a bigger role, India has devised many programmes and policies to improve critical supply chains, global health care, food and energy security, climate change mitigation, and reform of global governance institutions. India has shown to the world that there is something beyond the trade, technology and capital that are the driving force in a globalised economy, and that something is what the world currently lacks - that is, a new moral compass to enable humanity to recover from the ravages of the pandemic and prosper together.

Clean Energy

Today India is fast emerging as a global clean energy powerhouse. US Special Presidential Envoy for Climate Change John Kerry said India is an indisputable world leader in clean energy.[3] India announced that it aims to reach net zero emissions by 2070 and to meet fifty per cent of electricity requirements from renewable energy sources by 2030.[4] Prime Minister Narendra Modi has announced more ambitious targets for 2030, including installing 500 gigawatts of renewable energy capacity and reducing the emission intensity of its economy by 45 per cent.[5] India is also scaling up its footprints in emerging technologies such as hydrogen, battery storage, and low-carbon steel.

India's clean energy transition and global climate mitigation promises demonstrate the commitment of its leaders at the highest level. For instance, at COP26, in Glasgow, in November 2021, India expressed its intention to intensify its climate action by presenting an updated Nationally Determine Contributions (NDC). The update is a step toward India's long-term goal of reaching net-zero emissions by 2070.[6] At the Conference, Prime Minister Modi presented five nectar elements (*Panchamrit*) of climate action and his vision of sustainable lifestyles and climate justice to protect the poor and vulnerable everywhere from adverse impacts of climate change.[7] In Glasgow, Prime Minister Modi also proposed Mission LiFE, which would place individual behaviours at the centre of the global climate action narrative.[8] The Mission intends to establish and nurture a global network of individuals known as 'Pro-Planet People' (P3) committed to adopting and promoting environmentally friendly lifestyles.[9] This is a remarkable idea that appears simple but is profound in recognising that the root cause of climate change is individual behaviour, which when added up in a densely populated world, can cause incalculable damage to the environment and adversely impact the climate. Greed, rapacious materialism, unbridled consumption and profligate lifestyles have to be reviewed through introspection and their adverse effect mitigated through responsible national and international action.

Similarly, at the G7 Summit in June 2022, PM Modi highlighted India's efforts toward clean energy. He noted, "India has the world's first fully solar power operated airport. India's huge railway system will become net zero in this decade. We achieved the 40 per cent energy capacity target from non-fossil sources nine years before time".[10] Recently at the Global Clean Energy Action Forum 2022, in St Pittsburgh, USA, India emphasized the crucial role of Asia in decarbonisation initiatives.[11] This reaffirms India's commitment to working toward a low-carbon emission pathway while pursuing sustainable development goals.

Besides these multilateral commitments and proposals India has also signed bilateral clean energy partnership with EU, Japan and the US. For instance, during the Leaders' Summit on Climate, in April 2021, Prime Minister Modi and President Biden announced India-US Climate and Clean Energy Agenda 2030 Partnership, to accelerate progress toward shared climate and clean energy goals.[12] Taking this agenda forward both countries recently launched the Climate Action and Finance Mobilization Dialogue (CAFMD) and revamped the US-India Strategic Clean Energy Partnership (USISCEP).[13] A Ministerial dialogue of USISCEP, to be held on 7th October 2022. The partnership aims to advance energy security and innovation; scaling up emerging clean energy technologies; and deploying technical solutions through 5 pillars: *(i) Responsible Oil and Gas Pillar, (ii) Power and Energy Efficiency Pillar, (iii) Renewable Energy Pillar, (iv) Sustainable Growth Pillar, and (v) Emerging Fuels and technologies.*[14]

The India-Japan Clean Energy Partnership seeks to explore various options for ensuring a secure and stable supply of energy in order to achieve both the goals of sustainable economic growth and climate change mitigation. Cooperation under this partnership will cover areas including, Electric Vehicles (EV), storage systems including batteries, electric vehicle charging infrastructure (EVCI); Development of Solar Energy including Solar PV cells; Wind Energy; Clean, including Green Hydrogen; Clean, including Green Ammonia; Carbon Capture, Utilization & Storage (CCUS)/Carbon Recycling; Emerging fuels including Biofuels, CBG and Clean coal technology etc.[15]

The EU and India Clean Energy and Climate Partnership (CECP), was established in 2016. This aims to promote clean energy cooperation and the implementation of the Paris Agreement by increasing the deployment of climate-friendly energy sources such as solar and wind energy. Current areas of cooperation include activities in offshore wind energy, roof top solar and solar parks, integration of renewable energy and storage, smart grids, biofuels and energy efficiency in buildings. This partnership was reconfirmed in the joint statement at the EU-India Summit in October 2017[16] and later in July 2020 EU-India Strategic Partnership: A Roadmap to 2025 was agreed.[17]

India currently has around 99 gigawatts of installed renewable energy capacity, up from 35 gigawatts in 2014. Solar capacity is nearly 58 gigawatts, up from 2.6 gigawatts in 2014. Wind capacity increased to around

41 gigawatts from 21 gigawatts in the same period. Another 60 gigawatts is under various stages of implementation. By 2030, the Indian Renewable Sector is expected to create more than 3.4 million new jobs.[18] India has reported establishing five bioenergy centres. India, being one of the founding members of the Clean Energy Ministerial (CEM) will be hosting CEM-14 in 2023 Bengaluru along with its G20 presidency.

Critical Supply Chains

The globalization of supply chains was a defining feature of the pre-COVID world. However, the pandemic created a catastrophic spiral of protectionism and led to the subsequent breakdown of critical supply chains. Moreover, the future of global supply chains is becoming increasingly uncertain with rising geopolitical tensions. This crisis has presented an opportunity for India to emerge as a new fulcrum for multinational supply chains. It is in line with the *Make in India* initiative, which was launched in 2014 with the aim of making India a global manufacturing hub. *Make in India* encourages both multinational and domestic companies to produce their goods in India. In response to Covid-19, Prime Minister Modi launched the Atmanirbhar Bharat (Self-Reliant India Scheme) in May 2020. This scheme intends to make India more capable, more competitive, and more reliable as a trustworthy global supply chain hub. Speaking about Atmanirbhar Bharat at Davos Summit in 2021 PM Modi said that the programme "is committed to the global good and global supply chain. India has the capacity, capability and reliability to strengthen the global supply chain."[19]

Recently, the government launched National Logistics Policy (NLP) to improve the ease of doing business.[20] The policy aims to reduce the cost of logistics from 13-14%. This will boost the competitiveness of Indian products in both the domestic and international markets. When combined with previous connectivity and infrastructure improvement programmes such as the Gati Shakti Programme, Sagarmala, and Bharatmala, the NLP's transformational capabilities grow even more. Furthermore, India is taking steps to address the growing semiconductor crisis. For example, in December 2021, the government announced nearly $10 billion production-linked incentive (PLI) scheme to encourage chip manufacturing in India.[21] In March

2022, Union Cabinet approved the Semicon India program to develop the semiconductor and display manufacturing ecosystem. At the Semicon India Conference in April 2022, PM Modi said that the government aims to establish India as one of the key partners in global semiconductor supply chains. He said India has "an exceptional semiconductor design talent pool which makes up to 20% of the world's semiconductor design engineers."[22] Moreover, most of the top 25 semiconductor design companies have their design or R&D centres in our country.

Since the pandemic, India has also looked to bilateral and multilateral agreements to secure its own critical supply chains. For instance, In October 2021, at the G20 Summit PM Modi stressed on the need for resilient global supply chains. He also invited the G20 countries to make India their partner in economic recovery and supply chain diversification. Moreover, on the sidelines of the G20 Summit, Prime Minister participated in the Summit on 'Global Supply Chain Resilience' convened by US President Joe Biden. In the meeting, Modi underlined three critical aspects of "trusted source, transparency and time-frame" for improving global supply chains.[23] Furthermore, at the recent SCO Summit 2022, Modi called for a reliable supply chain in a meeting with Russian and Chinese presidents. Modi said that "the pandemic and the crisis in Ukraine have caused many disruptions in global supply chains, leaving the world facing unprecedented energy and food crises. Therefore, SCO should strive to develop reliable, resilient and diversified supply chains in our region."[24]

The trilateral Supply Chain Resilience Initiative launched in collaboration with Australia, and Japan is another significant step in addressing the supply chain crisis.[25] This initiative aims to coordinate and incentivize supply chain diversification away from China and toward the three countries and like-minded partners. Similarly, in September 2021, the Quadrilateral Security Forum (Quad) Leaders' Summit agreed that the four members would launch a Semiconductor Supply Chain Initiative to map and secure semiconductor supply chains.[26] In addition, the India-Japan Industrial Competitiveness Partnership (IJICP) also emphasized cooperation between the two nations in supply chain resilience.[27]

Digital Economy

Under Prime Minister Modi, India has emerged as one of the fastest-growing digital economies in the world. There has been rapid digitalisation in India in the past few years. The Covid-19 pandemic and the resultant lockdown have increased the scope of digital transactions in the country. The Ministry of Electronics and IT of India expressed the hope that India will have a digital economy worth one trillion by 2025-26. In addition, the expanding digital economy will be able to create 60-65 million job opportunities.

On 1 July 2015, PM Narendra Modi launched Digital India to transform India into an empowered digital economy.[28] Since then there has been a meteoric rise in mobile ownership across India in the last eight years. Access to mobiles increased from 15 per cent in 2014 to 66 per cent in 2022. The sharp decline in the cost of data has led to the deep penetration of the internet, bridging the urban-rural divide. While only 19 per cent of the population was connected to the internet in 2014, in 2020, it increased to 45 per cent. Digital India aims to increase the availability of the internet to Indian citizens and also to improve the digital infrastructure across the country.

The Government of India is also cooperating with tech giants worldwide to improve the 'Digital India Platform'. In 2019, GOI and Google launched the 'Build for digital India' program to help engineering graduates develop technology-based and market-ready solutions.[29] To promote research in quantum computing and its application, the Government of India has collaborated with Amazon Web Services since January 2021.[30] The Government of India is also cooperating with private companies like Google, Cognizant and Amazon to improve digital literacy in India.

Technology adoption by the government has also ensured a remarkable increase in transparency in governance. Today, almost all government programmes have a digital dashboard that provides all details of beneficiaries. For instance, the introduction of Direct Benefits Transfer and Aaadhaar authentication in various welfare schemes have eliminated ghost beneficiaries and ensured the timely delivery of benefits to citizens. As UPI has become the preferred mode of payment for all merchants, India is transitioning to a digital economy. The digital delivery of vaccines via the CoWIN platform enabled India to ensure vaccine equity and accessibility.

In 2021, India reported 48 billion real-time digital transactions, 40 per cent of the global total. Interestingly, which is nearly three times higher than China and seven times greater than the combined real-time payments volume of the world's leading economies – US, Canada, UK, France and Germany.[31]

India's digital transformation under Modi has not gone unnoticed. Around the world, there are countries have evinced interest in the Indian model of the UIDAI, Aadhar and the unified payments portals that link India's huge population into a seamless whole.

Healthcare

Healthcare is one of the priority areas of the Government of India and aims to make health care affordable for all. In 2021-22, India spent 2.1% of its GDP on public health compared to 1.8% in 2020-21. The compound annual growth rate of the health sector in India from 2016 to 2022 is around 22%. Over the years, the prospects of medical tourism in India have only increased. In 2020, the medical tourism market in India stood at USD 2.89 billion. It is expected to grow up to USD 13.42 billion by 2026. The prospects for telemedicine in India have also increased and are expected to grow to 5.5 billion by 2025.[32]

With India's expediency in the pharma sector and related supply chains, the world's third-largest start-up pool, there is a scope for exponential growth in this sector. Moreover, India can solve its healthcare problems with an increasing entrepreneurial spirit and more venture capital funds.

There are about 4.7 million people employed in India's health sector, which is one of the largest in the world. Since 2017, this sector has been creating 50,000 additional jobs every year.[33] Aiming at all ages and categories of people, the Government of India has developed various initiatives to provide access to healthcare. This includes the Pradhan Mantri Jan Arogya Yojana, Janani Suraksha Karyakram, Rashtriya Bal Swasthya Karyakram etc. For example, the Ayushman Bharat initiative provides comprehensive and need-based health care.

Now, India is a leading example and a hope for developing countries on account of its advanced technology in health security. Three aspects need to be understood:

(1) India believes in holistic development – the western notion of disease and medicine differs from the eastern version. India believes food and traditional practices like yoga as part of medicine that can promote the holistic development of an individual. PM Modi sought to promote this while proposing the International Day of Yoga by in his UNGA speech in 2014. Sharing the great Indian legacy of Yoga with the world was Modi's personal gift to humankind. Till then, Yoga was practices overseas in expensive studios and also subjected to all kinds of idiosyncratic interpretations, even made part of sporting competitions! Modi's initiative revived the true practise of Yoga in its purest form, making it available to the masses around the world, once again showing his feel for a "people connect". During COVID, the government promoted Ayurvedic medicine or simple home remedies to boost natural immunity. It is not an alternative to allopathic medicine but a complement to it.

(2) India's Philosophy and Health Crisis Management – Indian philosophy in dealing with health security focused on *Vasudhaiva Kutumbakam* means both that the world is important to us and that we are important to the world. Indian naval ship Kesari delivered food and medical assistance to the island nations of Maldives, Madagascar, Mauritius, Seychelles and Comoros in May 2020 – Mission SAGAR (Security and Growth for all in the Region).[34]

(3) The Indian initiatives were leading the discussion in WHO regarding delaying the intellectual property of vaccines. India exports medicines and other equipment to help other countries and became the first respondent in the Indian Ocean region. Vaccine Maitri helped deliver vaccines to 101 countries.[35] In addition, India has provided open-source apps like CoWIN and Arogya Sethu to other developing countries. The Modi government proclaimed these as Digital Public Good, which 50 countries have utilized for their vaccination drive. This is a true example of India's emergence as a *Vishwa Vaidya* or Global Physician.

Food, Fuel and Fertilizers

Today, global hunger is on the rise. According to a UN report, since Covid-19 breakout, over 150 million people have been added to the list of those affected by hunger.[36] India is the world's largest producer of milk and pulses.[37] Also, India is now the seventh largest exporter of agricultural products globally.[38] Over the last ten years, Indian agricultural exports have grown by just over eight times. Moreover, India is the top food supplier to the least developed countries (LDC), with around $5.2 billion in sales. This is nearly $1 billion more than the European Union and three times more than the United States exports to LDC.

India is also the largest producer of millet in the world. In 2018, India decided to mark the National Year of Millets. Later India pitched the proposal to the UN for declaring 2023 as the International Year of Millets, and the UNGA has recently declared 2023 as the International Year of Millets.[39]

As global food crisis triggered by the Ukraine war, many countries requested Indian wheat shipments. In February 2022, India signed an agreement with the WFP to distribute 50,000 metric tonnes of wheat to Afghanistan as humanitarian assistance.[40] India has also given Myanmar a shipment of 10,000 metric tonnes of rice and wheat.[41] In addition, the nation makes regular contributions to the World Food Programme, the Central Emergency Response Fund (CERF) of the UN, and the UN Office for the Coordination of Humanitarian Affairs (UNOCHA). India has set a target of 10 million tonnes of wheat in 2022-23 amid rising global grain demand because of the Russia-Ukraine conflict.[42] According to estimates by the Directorate General of Foreign Trade, India has exported a record 7 mt of wheat in 2021-22 which is valued at $ 2.05 billion.[43]

In the fertilisers industry, significant reforms have been put in place since 2014. These include gas-pooling,[44] which should boost domestic urea production efficiency, and neem-coating of urea, which has probably reduced the diversion of fertiliser intended for Indian farmers. Recently India introduced a one nation one fertilizer policy and taken decision of establishing brownfield urea manufacturing units through joint ventures.[45]

Regarding fertilizer exports, in 2022, India has agreed to export 1.2 lakh tonnes of urea and 50,000 tonnes of Di-Ammonnium Phosphate (DAP) to Nepal.[46] Similarly, 5,300 tonnes of DAP would be sent to Bhutan. India has also provided a $55 million line of credit to crisis-hit Sri Lanka for importing fertilizer, in a bid to help the island nation to address its worst economic hardships.[47] Despite a restriction on chemical fertiliser export, Sri Lanka would be the second country to get urea from India after Nepal.

India will be a significant benefactor of the emerging global energy trade in hydrogen, and the country might eventually become a net energy exporter. In order to export green hydrogen and establish hydrogen hubs in various locations around the nation, India can imitate the Australian models. Prime Minister Modi has said that India will become a worldwide centre for green hydrogen and that green hydrogen would provide India with a quantum leap in its efforts to combat climate change.

Disarmament and Non-Proliferation

India reiterates its commitment to the goal of a nuclear weapon-free world. It continues to prioritize and commit to universal, non-discriminatory, and verifiable nuclear disarmament. According to India's this objective can be attained through a step-by-step process supported by a shared commitment and an accepted global and non-discriminatory multilateral framework. In this regard, India is in favour of the Conference on Disarmament, the only multilateral disarmament negotiating mechanism operating on a consensus basis, starting talks on a comprehensive nuclear weapons convention. India did not take part in the 2017 Treaty on the Prohibition of Nuclear Weapons (TPNW) negotiations and has reaffirmed its refusal to become a party to the Treaty. This Treaty, according to India, does not create or contribute to the development of customary international law, nor does it establish any new standards or norms.[48]

In December 2017, India became the 42nd participating State in the Wassenaar Arrangement. Since then India actively participated the Experts Group meetings (April and September 2018), the General Working Group (May and October 2018) and the plenary (December 2018), with the aim of preventing proliferation of conventional arms and dual-use goods and technology.[49] In January 2018, India became a member of the Australia

Group as its 43rd partner and contributing to the realization of country's objectives of non-proliferation of chemical and biological weapons.[50]

India joined the Missile Technology Control Regime in June 2016 and has continued to participate in meetings of the Regime, including the technical expert group meetings held in Iceland in March and November 2018.[51] India joined and subscribed to The Hague Code of Conduct in June 2016. In compliance with the commitments on transparency and confidence-building measures, India has regularly notified The Hague Code of Conduct through pre-launch notifications of India's ballistic missile and space launches. India participated in the 17th meeting of The Hague Code of Conduct, held in Vienna on 28 and 29 May, 2018. India also submitted its annual declaration for 2018 and 2019.[52]

Regarding the Convention on the Prohibition of the Development, Production, Stockpiling and Use of Chemical Weapons and on Their Destruction, India continued to play an active role by engaging with States parties during various sessions of the Executive Council. India also offered to mentor Afghanistan under the mentorship programme of the Organisation for the Prohibition of Chemical Weapons.

Sustainability of Oceans

The Modi vision of hygiene and cleanliness is not limited to continental India. It includes the oceans too, where plastics waste and other polluting material have a trans-continental effect on everything, including the food chain and tourism. As a signatory of the UN "Coastal Clean Seas" campaign, India has undertaken several activities for achieving cleaner seas. On 17th September 2022, India conducted a cleanliness campaign, "Swachh Sagar, Surakshit Sagar/Clean Coast Safe Sea".[53] It is a 75-day citizen-led campaign for improving ocean health through collective action. Prime Minister Modi has also announced the intention to tackle plastic waste issue at the grass-roots level, phasing out single-use plastics by 2022.

In January, 2019, the Indian and Norwegian governments agreed to work more closely on oceans by signing a MoU and establishing the India-Norway Ocean Dialogue during the Norwegian Prime Minister's visit to India in January.[54] The agreement aims to share experiences and competence and collaborate on efforts to develop clean and healthy oceans, sustainable use of ocean resources and growth in the blue economy. In February 2022, India also signed an agreement with France to collaborate sustainable use of marine resources and to work towards ocean governance, including coordination in the relevant international bodies.[55]

Blue Economy Policy, Marine Spatial Planning (MSP), and Deep Ocean Mission (DOM) are some of the other significant major ocean initiatives taken by India recently.

Conclusion

These are some examples of the tremendous change in India's trajectory over the last eight years. India has now entered the period of "Amrit Kaal", which will provide a golden opportunity for India to achieve unprecedented levels of scientific, technological, economic and social progress by the time India celebrates centenary of its Independence. Under Prime Minister Modi's leadership, India has emerged as a responsible global power, willing to take on a leadership role in diverse areas. India's global stature has risen because it is willing to work today to deliver global public goods that benefits the entire world. India has shown initiative in this regard at a time when many other major countries are engaged in the pursuit of ideological or military confrontation, trade protectionism and technological contestation.

Endnotes

1. "Top UN official praises India for "thoughtful leadership and commitment" to advancing high-impact South South cooperation", *The Hindu*, October 8, 2022 at https://www.thehindu.com/news/international/top-un-official-praises-india-for-thoughtful-leadership-and-commitment-to-advancing-high-impact-south-south-cooperation/article65984119.ece
2. "Mexican President proposes global peace commission led by 3 leaders including PM Modi", *The Hindustan Times*, August 10, 2022 at https://www.hindustantimes.com/world-news/mexican-president-proposes-global-peace-commission-led-by-3-leaders-including-pm-modi-101660138477701.html
3. "India indisputably a world leader in deployment of renewable energy: John Kerry", *The Times of India*, April 6, 2021 at https://timesofindia.indiatimes.com/india/india-indisputably-a-world-leader-in-deployment-of-renewable-energy-john-kerry/articleshow/81935633.cms
4. "Cabinet approves India's Updated Nationally Determined Contribution to be communicated to the United Nations Framework Convention on Climate Change", *Press Information Bureau*, August 3, 2022 at https://pib.gov.in/PressReleaseIframePage.aspx?PRID=1847812

5. Ibid.
6. Ibid.
7. "National Statement by Prime Minister Shri Narendra Modi at COP26 Summit in Glasgow", *Press Information Bureau*, November 1, 2021 at https://pib.gov.in/PressReleasePage.aspx?PRID=1768712
8. "PM launches global initiative 'Lifestyle for the Environment - LiFE Movement", *Narendra Modi*, June 5, 2022 at https://www.narendramodi.in/prime-minister-narendra-modi-launches-life-movement-562392
9. Ibid.
10. "English Translation of Prime Minister's remarks at the session on 'Investing in a better Future: Climate, Energy, Health' at G7 Summit in Germany", *Ministry of External Affairs*, June 27, 2022 at https://www.mea.gov.in/Speeches-Statements.htm?dtl/35447/English_Translation_of_Prime_Ministers_remarks_at_the_session_on_Investing_in_a_better_Future_ Climate_ Energy_Health_at_G7_Summit_in_Germany
11. "Fact Sheet: United States Hosts First Ever Global Clean Energy Action Forum to Accelerate Clean Energy Innovation and Deployment" at chrome-extension://efaidnbmnnnibpcajpcglclefindmkaj/https://www.energy.gov/sites/default/files/2022-09/USG%20GCEAF%20FACTSHEET_final_1.pdf
12. "India-US Joint Statement on Launching the "India-US Climate and Clean Energy Agenda 2030 Partnership", *Ministry of External Affairs*, April 22, 2022 at https://mea.gov.in/bilateral-documents.htm?dtl/33821/IndiaUS+Joint+Statement+on+Launching+the+IndiaUS+Climate+ and+ Clean+Energy+Agenda+2030+Partnership
13. "India and US launch the Climate Action and Finance Mobilization Dialogue (CAFMD)", *Press Information Bureau*, September 13, 2021 at https://pib.gov.in/PressReleasePage.aspx?PRID=1754590
14. "Ministerial dialogue of US-India Strategic Clean Energy Partnership (USISCEP) to be held on 7th October 2022", *Press Information Bureau*, October 5, 2022 at https://pib.gov.in/PressReleaseIframePage.aspx?PRID=1865310
15. "India-Japan Clean Energy Partnership", *Ministry of External Affairs*, March 19, 2022 at https://www.mea.gov.in/bilateral-documents.htm?dtl/34992/IndiaJapan+Clean+Energy+Partnership
16. "EU-India Joint Statement on Clean Energy and Climate Change", at chrome-extension://efaidnbmnnnibpcajpcglclefindmkaj/https://www.consilium.europa.eu/media/23517/eu-india-joint-declaration-climate-and-energy.pdf
17. "EU-India Strategic Partnership: A Roadmap to 2025" at chrome-extension://efaidnbmnnnibpcajpcglclefindmkaj/https://www.consilium.europa.eu/media/45026/eu-india-roadmap-2025.pdf
18. "India's Expanding Clean Energy Workforce", at chrome-extension://efaidnbmnnnibpcajpcglclefindmkaj/https://www.nrdc.org/sites/default/files/indias-clean-energy-workforce-450-gw-target-report.pdf
19. "PM's address at the World Economic Forum's Davos Dialogue", *Narendra Modi*, January 28, 2021 at https://www.pmindia.gov.in/en/news_updates/pms-address-at-the-world-economic-forums-davos-dialogue/
20. "Logistics policy, a game-changer", *The New Indian Express*, October 19, 2022 at https://www.newindianexpress.com/opinions/2022/oct/19/logistics-policy-a-game-changer-2509533.html#:~:text=The%20National%20Logistics%20Policy%20(NLP,both%20domestic%20and%20international%20markets

21. "$10 billion production-linked incentive (PLI) scheme", *Mint*, December 16, 2021 at https://www.livemint.com/technology/tech-news/govt-rolls-out-10-bn-red-carpet-for-chipmakers-11639593541288.html
22. "PM inaugurates the Semicon India Conference 2022", *Press Information Bureau*, April 29, 2022 at https://pib.gov.in/PressReleasePage.aspx?PRID=1821165
23. "Prime Minister's address at Global Summit on Supply Chain Resilience", *Ministry of External Affairs*, October 31, 2021 at https://www.mea.gov.in/outoging-visit-detail.htm?34458/Prime+Ministers+address+at+Global+Summit+on+Supply+Chain+Resilience
24. "English Translation of Remarks by Prime Minister, Shri Narendra Modi at the SCO Summit", *Ministry of External Affairs*, September 16, 2022 at https://www.mea.gov.in/Speeches-Statements.htm?dtl/35719/English_Translation_of_Remarks_by_Prime_Minister_Shri_Narendra_Modi_at_the_SCO_Summit
25. "Australia-India-Japan Trade Ministers' Joint Statement on Launch of Supply Chain Resilience initiative", *Press Information Bureau*, April 27, 2021 at https://pib.gov.in/PressReleaseIframePage.aspx?PRID=1714362
26. "Fact Sheet: Quad Leaders' Summit", *Ministry of External Affairs*, September 24, 2021 at https://www.mea.gov.in/bilateral-documents.htm?dtl/34319/Fact+Sheet+Quad+Leaders+Summit
27. "India-Japan Summit Joint Statement Partnership for a Peaceful, Stable and Prosperous Post-COVID World", *Ministry of External Affairs*, March 19, 2022 at https://www.mea.gov.in/bilateral-documents.htm?dtl/34991/IndiaJapan+Summit+Joint+Statement+Partnership+ for+a+Peaceful+Stable+and+Prosperous+PostCOVID+World
28. "On 1 July 2015, PM Narendra Modi launched Digital India", *Live Mint*, June 29, 2021 at https://www.livemint.com/news/india/pm-modi-to-interact-with-beneficiaries-of-digital-india-on-july-1-11624976004176.html
29. "MeitY and Google tie up to Build for Digital India", *Digital India*, August 2019 at https://digitalindia.gov.in/content/meity-and-google-tie-build-digital-india
30. "Amazon Web Services is looking aggressively at the healthcare solutions sector, says top executive Max Peterson", *Business Today*, June 16, 2022 at https://www.businesstoday.in/latest/corporate/story/amazon-web-services-is-looking-aggressively-at-the-healthcare-solutions-sector-says-top-executive-max-peterson-337930-2022-06-16
31. "India Surges Ahead as the World's Leader in Real-Time Payments – Boosting Economic Growth – ACI Worldwide Report", *ACI Worldwide*, April 26, 2022 at https://investor.aciworldwide.com/news-releases/news-release-details/india-surges-ahead-worlds-leader-real-time-payments-boosting
32. "Healthcare Industry in India", *IBEF* at https://www.ibef.org/industry/healthcare-india
33. Ibid.
34. "Under Mission Sagar, INS Kesari delivers 500 tonnes of food aid to Mozambique", *The Hindustan Times*, December 26, 2021 at https://www.hindustantimes.com/india-news/under-mission-sagar-ins-kesari-delivers-500-tonnes-of-food-aid-to-mozambique-101640509490655.html
35. "Vaccine Supply", *Ministry of External Affairs* at https://mea.gov.in/vaccine-supply.htm
36. "UN Report: Global hunger numbers rose to as many as 828 million in 2021", *WHO*, July 6, 2022 at https://www.who.int/news/item/06-07-2022-un-report—global-hunger-numbers-rose-to-as-many-as-828-million-in-2021
37. "India at a glance", *FAO* at https://www.fao.org/india/fao-in-india/india-at-a-glance/en/#:~:text=India%20is%20the%20world's%20largest,%2C%20vegetables%2C%20fruit%20and%20cotton

38. Ibid.
39. "United Nations declares 2023 International Year of Millets", *The Hindu*, April 27, 2021 at https://www.thehindu.com/news/national/karnataka/united-nations-declares-2023-international-year-of-millets/article34418239.ece
40. "India and WFP sign MoU for final tranche of wheat donation to the people of Afghanistan", *WFP*, July 11, 2022 at https://www.wfp.org/news/india-and-wfp-sign-mou-final-tranche-wheat-donation-people-afghanistan
41. "India provides 10 lakh doses of Covid-19 vaccines, 10,000 tonnes of rice and wheat to Myanmar", *The Times of India*, December 23, 2021 at https://timesofindia.indiatimes.com/india/india-provides-10-lakh-doses-of-covid-19-vaccines-10000-tonnes-of-rice-and-wheat-to-myanmar/articleshow/88450693.cms
42. "India aims to export 10 million tonne of wheat worth $4 billion in 2022-23", Financial Express, April 4, 2022 at https://www.financialexpress.com/economy/india-aims-to-export-10-million-tonne-of-wheat-worth-4-billion-in-2022-23/2480352/
43. "India's wheat exports prospects get boost, with Egypt agreeing to import grain", *Press Information Bureau*, April 15, 2022 at https://pib.gov.in/PressReleaseIframePage.aspx?PRID=1817118
44. "Pooling of Gas in Fertilizer (Urea) Sector", *Press Information Bureau*, March 31, 2015 at https://pib.gov.in/newsite/printrelease.aspx?relid=117888
45. "Modi launches 'Bharat' under 'one nation, one fertiliser' plan", *The Times of India*, October 18, 2022 at https://timesofindia.indiatimes.com/india/modi-launches-bharat-under-one-nation-one-fertiliser-plan/articleshow/94927632.cms
46. "India to export urea, DAP to Nepal, Sri Lanka", *The Times of India*, may 18, 2022 at https://timesofindia.indiatimes.com/india/india-to-export-urea-dap-to-nepal-sri-lanka/articleshow/91628727.cms
47. Ibid.
48. "India's view on the Treaty on the Prohibition of Nuclear Weapons", *Ministry of External Affairs*, January 22, 2021 at https://mea.gov.in/press-releases.htm?dtl/33409/Indias+view+on+the+Treaty+on+the+Prohibition+of+Nuclear+Weapons
49. "India Joins the Wassenaar Arrangement", *Ministry of External Affairs*, December 8, 2017 at https://www.mea.gov.in/press-releases.htm?dtl/29164/India_Joins_the_ Wassenaar_ Arrangement
50. "India Joins Australia Group" at https://www.armscontrol.org/act/2018-03/news-briefs/india-joins-australia-group
51. "Note verbale dated 21 August 2019 from the Permanent Mission of India to the United Nations addressed to the Chair of the Committee", *Ministry of External* Affairs, August 22, 2019 at https://www.mea.gov.in/Portal/Images/S-AC-44-2019-7-E-India-UNSC-1540-2019-Report.pdf
52. Ibid.
53. "Swachh Sagar, Surakshit Sagar/Clean Coast Safe Sea", *Press Information Bureau*, August 27, 2022 at https://pib.gov.in/PressReleasePage.aspx?PRID=1854856
54. "Joint Statement during the State Visit of Prime Minister of Norway to India (January 08, 2019)", *Ministry of External Affairs*, January 8, 2019 at https://mea.gov.in/bilateral-documents.htm?dtl/30894/Joint_Statement_during_the_State_Visit_of_ Prime_ Minister_of_Norway_to_India_January_08_2019
55. "India-France Roadmap on the Blue Economy and Ocean Governance", *Ministry of External Affairs*, February 20, 2022 at https://www.mea.gov.in/bilateral-documents.htm?dtl/34882/

8

Positive Foreign Policy of Prime Minister Modi

Harsh Vardhan Shringla

The international order is currently passing through a phase of severe stress. The pandemic was probably the harshest global shock in living memory. Even as we began to emerge from it, we were confronted with a major geopolitical challenge that arose from the conflict between Russia and Ukraine. The impact of this conflict, and the continuing trauma of the pandemic, has combined with the lingering consequences of the 2008 economic crisis to produce a set of interlocking stresses. These stresses are manifesting inter alia as negative macroeconomic trends, financial collapses and defaults, including in our neighbourhood, energy crises, food shortages, and, supply chain failures.

World leaders have to deal with these challenges while they navigate technological disruptions, extreme climate events, and a world in transition in which the centre of geopolitical, geo-economic and increasingly, geotechnical gravity shifts towards Asia.

Stresses and uncertainties of this magnitude call for global responses. They also call for visionary leadership and for great qualities of statesmanship. Prime Minister Narendra Modi's New India has demonstrated these qualities as he steered India through this storm. He has also turned India into one of the few bright spots on the global landscape. It is an India that is resilient, reacts rapidly, and innovates. It is an India that has bounced back to become one of the fastest growing global economies. It is also an India that did not hesitate, in the most difficult of times, to share its resources and its capacities, for the greater global good.

Prime Minister Narendra Modi has been at the forefront of international diplomacy in these times of uncertainty and flux. India is currently serving a non-permanent tenure in the UN Security Council. Prime Minister Modi has been present at all G7 summits in the last few years. He is about to lead India into its first ever G20 Presidency. He has anchored greater Indian involvement in the QUAD. His role in the Shanghai Cooperation Organisation, which India will also chair, has received global attention. He played a remarkable role as a thought leader and a man of action during the Climate Change COP 26 Summit.

He, and India, have thus risen to the challenge of these times.

This is not an accident. Prime Minister Modi has meticulously, and indefatigably, created a new paradigm in foreign and strategic policies since 2014. He has created an intellectual framework and imparted direction to these policies through the civilizational concept of "Vasudaiva Kutumbakam"; through the soaring vision of 'Sabka Saath, Sabka Vikas, Sabka Vishwas' and now, 'Sabka Prayas'; through the call for a "human-centric globalization"; and through far-sighted policies such as SAGAR—Security and Growth for All in the Region.

His tireless efforts at outreach, in person, and through innovative digital means, such as virtual summits, have created unprecedented global interest in India. He has created a better international economic reality for India through a new generation of regional trade agreements, through green strategic partnerships, through 21st century mobility and migration agreements, and, through technology and innovation partnerships. These have led, among other things, to the highest ever levels of exports and FDI in our history.

The International Day of Yoga, entirely conceived by him, is a global movement. His call for sustainable lifestyles, for "One World, One Health", and his promotion of Ayurveda are certain to have far-reaching impacts. The organization of 'Azadi ka Amrit Mahotsav' on a global scale demonstrates his unmatched understanding of the dynamics of soft power.

Prime Minister Modi has also directed a major operational transformation in Indian foreign policy. He has placed emphasis on Neighbourhood First. This has meant more frequent contacts at the highest level than ever before; transformed connectivity and economic linkages; greater movement of goods, services, ideas and people; and forward-looking cooperation.

India is a net provider of security in its immediate and extended neighbourhood. It has created maritime domain awareness networks, increased joint and coordinated surveillance operations and patrols with other countries, and augmented the security infrastructure of its partners. Platforms such as the Colombo Security Conclave have created new opportunities for cooperation in this area.

India is also an acknowledged first responder. Prime Minister Modi has extended India's helping hand and healing touch after natural and humanitarian disasters in an arc that extends from Banda Aceh in Indonesia all the way across the Indian Ocean to Mozambique and Madagascar. In the neighbourhood, Indian HADR capacities were rapidly and effectively deployed following the Nepal earthquake, in Bangladesh, in Sri Lanka, and in the Maldives.

India has become a major source of finance and investments in the neighbourhood. Lines of credit to its neighbours have jumped from US$ 3 billion in 2014 to almost US$ 15 billion in 2022.

Tens and thousands of students from neighbouring countries are enrolled in Indian institutions ranging from primary schools to super-specialized training institutions. The New Education Policy crafted under Prime Minister's stewardship will build a 21st century education and skilling infrastructure which will make India a global education hub.

Perhaps nothing captures the spirit of this new engagement with our neighbours as much as the invitation to Prime Minister Modi to join Bangladesh's celebrations of the 50th year of its independence in 2021.

This is evidence of success in overcoming the hesitations of history.

Prime Minister Modi has also been resolute and unflagging in countering the challenge of terrorism. He has demonstrated resolve, and results, through the creation of capacities and through alliances and networks based on multilateral and pluri-lateral constructs such as the UN and FATF, and closer home, through BIMSTEC, BBIN, IORA, SCO RATS, and IONS.

India was firm in its response to Chinese aggression along the Line of Actual Control in Ladakh in 2020. Sixteen rounds of talks at the level of military commander have resolved many of the issues arising out of this adventurism by China. However, the message is clear. Peace and tranquillity in the border areas is an essential prerequisite for the development of our bilateral relationships. External Affairs Minister, Dr. S. Jaishankar, has emphasized that the development of India-China relations has to be based on 'three mutuals'—mutual respect, mutual sensitivity and mutual interest.

Even as Prime Minister Modi has placed the Neighbourhood First, he has ensured that we Act East and we Think West. He has revitalized our approach to these policies. His Act East policies have created the ground for Indian engagement in the critical Indo-Pacific construct. The Indo-Pacific is not just a geographical expression. It is the new epicentre of global politics and global economics with 60 per cent of the world's population, two-thirds of the global economic output and more than half of global trade transiting through its waters.

His relationship with leaders of the Arab world and in the Gulf region has fundamentally altered geopolitical dynamics and created better realities for India. Exciting initiatives such as the I2U2 are creating new alignments that will generate concrete outcomes.

India's relations with major powers have attained comprehensive strategic levels while maintaining strategic autonomy. We have carefully tended our relationship with the USA. It is an exciting and forward-looking partnership which Prime Minister Modi has personally cultivated. He is presiding over a transformation of our relations with Europe and the United Kingdom based on economic and technological complementarities, on shared values and through new alignments such as the India-Nordic summit.

Prime Minister Modi is the pre-eminent leader of the global South and of the developing world. He has ensured growing and more meaningful engagement with developing countries. He is a welcome visitor in Africa, which he has engaged inter alia through the India Africa Forum Summit. He has brought India closer to Indian Ocean island countries. He has engaged with the Pacific Island countries through the Pacific Islands Forum Summit; and with the Caribbean through the India-CARICOM Meet.

Prime Minister Modi is also determined to make India a force for good in international affairs. Nothing demonstrates this better than his role at the forefront of the international response to the COVID-19 pandemic. Recognizing that the virus was not constrained by borders, he mobilized South Asian leaders, and larger multilateral platforms, such as the G20, to combat the crisis. He also unhesitatingly deployed India's capacities in the service of humanity during this battle.

The lockdowns stranded millions of Indians across the globe. They were brought home through Vande Bharat, the largest evacuation exercise in history in the face of daunting logistical challenges. The Prime Minister personally supervised this herculean effort.

He turned India into the pharmacy of the world, supplying critical pharma products and medical supplies to more than 150 countries in the world.

Indian medical capacities were deployed in its extended neighbourhood through rapid response teams and HADR operations such as Operation Sagar.

"Vaccine Maitri", one of his most courageous and far-sighted decisions, in very difficult circumstances, established India's credentials as a leading healthcare hub with advanced capacities. More importantly, it established India as a reliable and dependable partner.

This goodwill ensured that India received global help when it was ravaged by the second wave of the pandemic.

His call for a new template of globalization, based on fairness, equality and humanity in the post-COVID world, was thus well-received internationally.

The Prime Minister also placed India, in response to the realities of lockdowns and supply chain disruptions, on the path to Atmanirbharata. This has turned out to be the basis for a new economic diplomacy in which India is increasingly in the focus of global supply chains and value chains. The high FDI inflows and growth in manufacturing demonstrate that his vision is paying economic dividends.

The massive effort to augment indigenous defence capabilities and create the framework for private sector participation in the space industry, both propelled by the Prime Minister, will have far-reaching impacts.

Prime Minister Narendra Modi has single-handedly shifted India's standing in the Climate Change conversation. His commitment to leadership by action has ensured that India is one of the few countries that has been unwavering in complying with the Paris Agreement commitments. He has placed India on the path to becoming one of the world's largest renewable electricity producers. The International Solar Alliance (ISA), which has created a platform of 121 partner countries to promote the development of solar energy projects worldwide, is his creation. He has also taken the lead in launching the Coalition for Disaster Resilient Infrastructure (CDRI). His Panchamrit, announced at COP 26, the National Hydrogen Mission and his concept of LIFE (Lifestyle for Environment) will ensure that India is in the front rank of countries with climate ambitions. India, for its own reasons, has been a part of the solution, and not the problem, in this preeminent global challenge of our times.

India has, under his leadership, become a major development partner with operations in more than 50 countries in five continents. He has exported Indian values by constructing parliaments, hospitals, infrastructure projects, and educational institutes across the world. He has also focused on digital enablers such as the United Payment Interface, the Co-Win app, and Aadhaar; and such initiatives such as Jal Jeevan which will create goodwill for India and place cutting-edge Indian prowess at the disposal of its partners in a transformed global environment.

While doing this, Prime Minister Modi has ensured that Indian foreign policy is not confined to an ivory tower. He has mobilized the Indian Diaspora into a great global community. He has electrified the Indian population abroad and connected it to India through events such as Howdy Modi in the USA, and through interactions in the UK, UAE and other major concentrations of overseas and non-resident Indians.

Indian consular operations have been transformed at his instance. Electronic platforms and portals are being utilized to provide class-leading standards of consular service across the world.

Prime Minister Modi has ensured that no Indian is left behind when disaster strikes. Most recently, 23,000 Indian students were evacuated from Ukraine through a complicated mission called 'Operation Ganga'. Another evacuation operation, 'Operation Devi Shakti', was launched when crisis enveloped Afghanistan.

To conclude, there is no doubt that India has, under Prime Minister Modi's leadership, shifted gears and moved on to a trajectory that will take it to greater heights and to the front ranks of the international community. In doing so, he has created a new paradigm for leadership at the international level that draws from India's civilizational heritage and strengths, and works towards making the world a truly better place.

9

The India-ASEAN Relationship and PM Modi's Contribution

Anil Wadhwa

India's "Look East Policy" was introduced in the 1990s and was transformed in 2015 to the "Act East Policy" by Prime Minister Modi. India's 'Act East' policy is now firmly focused on stronger commercial links with the ASEAN and other Indo-Pacific countries and to create opportunities for the connectivity and development of the Indian North-eastern states. The year 2022 marked the thirtieth anniversary of dialogue relations between ASEAN and India and was celebrated as the ASEAN–India 'Friendship Year'. On 15 June 2022, India hosted the Special ASEAN-India foreign ministers' meeting to mark the thirtieth anniversary of its dialogue relations and the tenth anniversary of its strategic partnership with ASEAN. Prime Minister Modi has recognized the ASEAN as a vital component of the regional and global multilateral order and supports its central position in the developing Indo-Pacific region. PM Modi's recognition of the centrality of ASEAN is in alignment with his vision of the "Indo-Pacific". India does not view the Indo-Pacific as a strategy or a club of limited members but as an inclusive, natural region ranging from the shores of Africa to that of the Americas. Prime Minister Modi, speaking at the Shangri-La Dialogue in Singapore in 2018, had stated that the Indo–Pacific should be "free, open and inclusive", grounded in "rules and norms" based on the consent of all, not on the 'power of a few', and characterized by respect for international law, including the issue of freedom of navigation and overflight. On this occasion, PM Modi also pointed out that it was ASEAN that had laid the foundation of the Indo-Pacific region, and key ASEAN initiatives embrace its geography by including India. Therefore, rather than being divisive or dismissive, India's vision for the Indo–Pacific further reassures and reinforces the ASEAN. Over the past few decades, India has made important progress in its relationship with ASEAN and its related frameworks. India was a dialogue partner in 1996 became a summit-level partner in 2002, a strategic partner in 2012 and has since reached the level of a comprehensive strategic partner at the thirtieth India-ASEAN Commemorative Summit in November 2022. Today, India is engaged in at least 30 high-level dialogues at the ministerial level in diversified fields with ASEAN. India has also been an active participant in the East Asia Summit, and its related security and economic groupings like ARF (ASEAN Regional Forum) and ADMM+ (ASEAN Defence Ministers Plus), which have many overlaps in membership. India's relationship with ASEAN encompasses many aspects, including the political, security, economic, cultural and people-to-people dimensions.

India has always hailed the deep cultural and civilizational ties that have existed between India and the ASEAN countries. This relationship dates back to ancient times, when India had a significant influence on the cultures of South-East Asia, particularly through the spread of Hinduism and Buddhism. In ASEAN countries like Cambodia, Indonesia or Myanmar today, many symbolic remnants of India's influence are clearly visible in their art, culture and civilization. Through the centuries, India has been a source of inspiration for art and architecture in countries belonging to the present-day ASEAN. Indian religion, political thought, literature, mythology, artistic motifs and style, were absorbed deeply into local culture as greater interaction with Indians who settled in South-East Asia took place. Buddhism came to South-East Asia from India in the third century BCE when Buddhist monks were sent as emissaries by king Ashoka. India has had a significant influence on the food and flavours of South-East Asia, as there are many common spices in Indian and South-East Asian cuisines. In addition, Indian herbal medicines have been used in South-East Asia for centuries and continue to be popular in many countries.

Prime Minister Modi also sought to provide the relationship with ASEAN a direction of economic integration, market access, investment and trade, besides emphasizing the age-old cultural and people-to-people ties. The reason why India needs deeper economic integration with ASEAN and needs to engage it actively is because it consists of 1.85 billion people, and has a combined GDP of $ 3.8 trillion. The ASEAN India Trade in Goods Agreement, the ASEAN India Trade in Services Agreement and the ASEAN India Investment Agreement are in force, and have been ratified by all parties. Bilateral trade has risen, reaching US$ 98.39 billion in 2021-22, even though the pace could have been faster. PM Modi sensed that this area requires much more attention, and the creation of new and resilient supply chains between India and ASEAN with focus on digital trade would bring down costs. This needs to be bolstered by a review of the ASEAN India Agreement on Trade if India has to benefit equally from the Agreement. A revamped India ASEAN Free Trade Agreement will compensate to a large extent for India not being part of the Regional Comprehensive Economic Cooperation Agreement (RCEP). The Indo-Pacific Economic Framework, launched by the USA in May 2022, which includes India and seven ASEAN countries, will also help in taking the economic agenda of India and ASEAN forward. ASEAN has invested US$ 117.88 billion between April 2000 and February 2022 in India, and India has invested US$ 55.5 billion in ASEAN between April 2019 and March 2022. Investment flows, however, are predominantly to and from Singapore, and there is a need for diversification and expansion of investments with a host of other ASEAN countries.

Connectivity is a key aspect of improving the economic relationship with ASEAN through land, sea, and air. India and ASEAN will benefit both if the construction of the trilateral highway which will connect India, Myanmar and Thailand, and will later expand into Laos, Cambodia and Vietnam is speeded up and completed in the near future. Currently, it is bogged in political, financial and governance constraints in Myanmar.PM Modi's vision for India– ASEAN relations is anchored in the shared values of democracy, pluralism and economic prosperity. PM Modi sees ASEAN as crucial to the success of India's 'Act East' policy. He has therefore sought to elevate this partnership through high-level meetings, senior-level visits, as well as multilateral initiatives leading to strengthening economic ties.

A $ 1 billion credit line was announced by PM Modi in 2015 to enhance digital and infrastructure connectivity with ASEAN. Over $ 77 million have also been committed towards developing manufacturing hubs in the CML (Cambodia, Myanmar and Laos) countries. The soft infrastructure required for the successful opening of the trilateral highway, including a motor vehicles and licensing agreement, customs checkpoints and documentation, as well as economic hubs along the highway, must be in place when the trilateral highway opens. This is essential because the North-east itself must be able to export its produce and benefit economically rather than becoming just an importer of cheap goods. Most urgently, connectivity development in the Northeast is important so that India can hope for balanced trade and utilize the full potential of its North-eastern states.

The Kaladan multi-modal transport project will link Kolkata to Sittwe port in Myanmar, extending into Mizoram by the river and land route. This project, again, has been stuck for a while due to the political situation in Myanmar. India's involvement and the idea of developing port infrastructure in Sabang is significant and could be a game changer but needs quicker follow up. Sea links are also vital between the eastern seaboard of India including the ports of Ennore and Chennai to CML countries and there is a need for improving trans-shipment links with partners like Malaysia, Singapore, Indonesia and Thailand. Experimental routes have been tried and have turned out to be promising. These need to be scaled up. There is a proposal to link Dawei port in Myanmar, being developed with Japan and Thailand, to Chennai port in India. However, Japan, Thailand and Myanmar all need to come together with India with finance and ideas in order that this proposal fructifies and succeeds. India and ASEAN also need to look at shipping joint ventures, and related concessions through an agreement on maritime transport. While flight connections from tier-1 and tier-2 cities in India are well established with Singapore, Thailand, Malaysia and now Indonesia, the other countries either lack direct links or have inadequate linkages with India. This is an impediment to tourism, as well as trade and investments. India and ASEAN, therefore, need to work towards an ASEAN-India comprehensive air services agreement which will benefit trade, investments and tourism.

India has constantly promoted centrality and striven to build the capacity of ASEAN to the best of its ability. Mutually beneficial cooperative activities are one primary means of engagement, and these joint activities are identified either as part of a five-year "plan of action" or through the "Work Plans" of cooperation generated during interactions with ASEAN "sectoral bodies" or institutions. India is also looking to partner with ASEAN in enhancing blue economy cooperation, investing in development of desalinization technologies, harvesting bio-diversity, and searching for and excavating marine minerals in the seas. India is setting up coastal surveillance networks and constantly enhancing the capacity for a shared maritime domain awareness with its partners. India has concentrated on defence arrangements at a bilateral level, strengthening defence ties with countries like Singapore, Vietnam, Indonesia, Malaysia, Philippines, Myanmar and Thailand. India carries out maritime exercises with countries like Singapore and Indonesia, and the Indian navy conducts the Milan exercise with navies of the Indian Ocean Region at the Andaman and Nicobar Islands. India and Singapore already have an agreement for the mutual logistics pact which was signed a few years ago and helps in the Indian navy's operational turnaround. The first ever ASEAN-India maritime exercise is scheduled to take place in the first quarter of 2023, where the focus is expected to be on interoperability and exchange of best practices amongst all the navies.

Besides the $ 50-million ASEAN-India Cooperation Fund (later augmented in 2016 by another US$ 50 million by Prime Minister Modi), India has set up a $ 1-million Green Fund (later augmented to $ 5 million) which helps in undertaking cooperative projects in climate impact mitigation. In 2016, the corpus of the fund meant for enhancing science and technology with ASEAN was also enhanced by India from $ 1 million to US$ 5 million. Two major space projects with ASEAN for tracking, data and reception/ data processing stations are located Ho Chi Minh city, Vietnam, and in Biak, Indonesia. India is working to enhance cooperation with ASEAN in digitization—especially the financial structure and e-governance as well as cyber security. India is ideally placed to use its niche area in IT to power customs and risk management. India and its partners like Japan, Australia or the USA who are part of the "Quad" could partner other governments or the private sector to mitigate risk and shorten lead times in the region. The Comprehensive Strategic Partnership with ASEAN would enhance cooperation in areas like energy, health, investment in "Make in India" programmes, technology, and climate change mitigation. Collaboration in areas such as financial technology, connectivity, start-ups, and innovation, empowerment of youth and women and the development of micro, small and medium enterprises will be an important driver in moving India-ASEAN relations to a higher pedestal.

Prime Minister Modi has also supported the idea of an ASEAN community, which aims to integrate the economies, politics and culture of the member-countries. To this end, India has been imparting training in the English language, IT, law enforcement and capital market skills to personnel in countries like Laos, Cambodia and Myanmar. Scholarships have been offered in Nalanda University, and training of civil servants in disaster risk management and drought management, as well as exchange of parliamentarians has been carried out. There has been the establishment of a network of think tanks, ASEAN-India eminent persons lecture series, ASEAN-India students exchange programmes, and an ASEAN-India media exchange programme.

Prime Minister Modi is also the pioneer of the Indo-Pacific Oceans Initiative (IPOI). It is also part of the Security and Growth for All (SAGAR) mission to expand and facilitate regional cooperation of India's maritime resources. The objective of the Indo-Pacific Oceans initiative is to strengthen maritime boundaries, and to this end, partnerships based on principles of free trade and sustainable use of maritime resources have been proposed. Such partnerships have three main goals in the Indian Ocean region—wealth creation, welfare promotion, and cooperative win-win strategies. The Initiative draws upon regional architecture and mechanisms to focus on seven pillars of maritime security, maritime ecology, maritime resources, capacity building and resource sharing, disaster risk reduction and management, science, technology and academic cooperation, as well as trade connectivity and maritime transport. The elevation of ties should ensure greater coordination between India's IPOI and ASEAN's outlook on the Indo-Pacific (AOIP). The ASEAN outlook on the Indo-Pacific is aimed at promoting an enabling environment for peace, stability and prosperity in the region in addressing common challenges, upholding the rule-based regional architecture, and promoting closer economic cooperation, thus strengthening confidence and trust. It also aims at implementing existing and exploring other ASEAN priority areas of cooperation, including maritime cooperation, connectivity, the sustainable development goals, and economic and other possible areas of cooperation. Most importantly, India needs to present itself as a viable alternative to other partners in the ASEAN economic and strategic landscape. For this, India will have to be focused on completing its connectivity projects with ASEAN, make continuous efforts to develop better defence, cultural, and socio-economic ties, and continue to strengthen interdependencies with the countries of the ASEAN. Prime Minister Modi is fully supportive and committed to strengthening this relationship further.

10

India Now Has an Answer for Cross-Border Terror

Ajay Bisaria

Three-quarters of a century after the two countries got independence, Pakistan remains a key security challenge for India. After failing in three major wars (in 1947-48, 1965 and 1971), two of them initiated by it to acquire territory in Kashmir, Pakistan's military establishment fashioned-and honed a sub-conventional dagger to run through India's internal fissures. This was the instrument of state-sponsored terrorism, designed in the 1970s, to bleed India slowly. By launching proxy terror wars in two border states—in Punjab from the 1980s and in Jammu & Kashmir from the 1990s—Pakistan emerged as both an external and internal security challenge for India.

While the growing military power differential gave India a clear advantage in the conventional realm, the country had no good answer for the sub-conventional proxy terror that visited its territory. India had no clear red lines to deter this imported terror, as the threshold of tolerance remained ambiguous and was thus continually tested. Terror traumatised not just the border states of Punjab and J&K, but also regions beyond; it brazenly spread its tentacles deeply affecting the psyche of an entire nation. Only in the seventh decade after independence could India summon the will and the instruments to credibly take on the crippling challenge of external terrorism. With the arrival in 2014 of a new government led by Prime Minister Narendra Modi, India's policy makers were finally willing to tackle imported terror with a comprehensive cross-border response.

The BJP-led government was always expected to be tough on terror and even tougher on Pakistan. Defying expectations, however, the government began with a peace overture to its western neighbour by inviting Pakistan's then Prime Minister, Nawaz Sharif, to India for the swearing-in ceremony of Prime Minister Modi in May 2014. Just eighteen months later, PM Modi himself paid a return visit to Lahore (in December 2015), expending considerable personal political capital in the enterprise.

However, within a week of the Indian Prime Minister's visit, a terror attack on the Pathankot Air Force Station in northern Punjab, by suspected Jaish-e-Mohammed (JeM) militants, validated the pessimistic assessment that high-level engagement with Pakistan mostly served as an invitation for a terror backlash.

An attack on an Indian army camp in Kashmir's Uri in 2016 proved to be the last straw. Behind the September attacks was again the JeM, now the ISI's weapon of choice (since its other protégé, the Lashkar-e-Taiba (LeT) was facing the heat since its 2008 Mumbai attacks). The response from India came swiftly. The Indian Army's 2016 surgical strikes—multiple attacks on terrorist launch pads across the LOC—signalled to Pakistan that in dealing with cross-border terror, India was now ending the era of handling proxy warfare with strategic restraint, replacing it with a posture of 'offensive defence', a willingness to respond beyond its borders and with public disclosure.

The air strikes of 2019, in response to the JeM's massive Pulwama terror attack of 14 February, reaffirmed this resolve. The signal to Pakistan, as also to the global community, was clear. India was now ready for hot pursuit, for crossing the LOC, or even the international boundary, to check terrorism at its home base. This response from its larger adversary to punitively or pre-emptively challenge terror at its source now entered Pakistan's security calculus. Pakistan had a clear 'assurance' that India's response to acts of terrorism above a certain threshold would not only be proportionate and punitive, but could also be massive and pre-emptive. In effect, India's broader response implied a policy of reduced tolerance of terror, commensurate with, as could be expected in an effective democracy, a lowering of the threshold of public acceptance of terrorism. Reacting to terror attacks in Jammu & Kashmir, India put in place an effective counterterrorism grid within the territory, bolstered by a 'forward policy' of tackling terrorism deep within Pakistan. The CT policy was accompanied by a diplomatic posture since 2016 of curtailing structured engagement with Pakistan, popularly dubbed the phase of 'no talks with terror'.

A History of Mounting Terror

Barely two months after both countries achieved independence, Pakistan launched a proxy war against India, the earliest jihad, deploying hordes of militant Kabaili Pathan warriors, the 'raiders of Kashmir', who marched towards Srinagar from the border district of Rajouri, with a brutal agenda of occupation, rape and pillage. The move triggered the formal accession of the princely state of Jammu and Kashmir into the nascent Indian Union on 26 October, 1947. The war of 1947-48 became the first experiment by Pakistan in asymmetric warfare with deniable state involvement.

In the first quarter century of independence, Pakistan tried to impose direct military solutions to realise its irredentist goals. In the past four decades, however, it relied mostly on proxy terror. Cross-border terrorism itself has broadly gone through four phases: the Punjab phase of the 80s; the Kashmir phase of the 90s; the all-India phase under the nuclear umbrella from 1998; and the cautious phase from 2008, under the shadow of the FATF.

The Punjab Phase

The ISI's early experiences in the Afghanistan of the 1970s had emboldened it to attempt an insurgency in India beyond Kashmir. Punjab seemed ripe for the picking. It proved an irresistible option for Pakistan's military, still licking its wounds after the humiliation of the severing of its eastern wing in 1971. Pakistan's ISI learnt the art of effectively fomenting and supporting an insurgency that would cause deep pain to India through the 80s. Pakistan would simply run an inexpensive dagger through India's existing fault-lines.

Both history and geography played a role. The troubled waters of Punjab—the land of the five rivers—gave Pakistan an opportunity to fish at a time when it did not want to confront India militarily and was engaged in US-sponsored military action on its own western border in Afghanistan, then an active frontier of the Cold War. Fanning the flames of insurgencies in Punjab (and later in Kashmir) seemed like a great tactic to the ISI. In fact, this was a unique opportunity for Pakistan to fight the next battle for territory from behind the scenes through covert operations cloaked in deniability.

Pakistan's interest in Khalistan went beyond revenge. It became a tactical goal. This interest intensified with Bhutto's successor, General Zia-ul-Haq. It had been clear to both Bhutto and Zia that since Pakistan could not reasonably expect conventional parity with India, it had to find a newer strategic doctrine covering a broad spectrum of warfare: an edge in sub-conventional warfare that India would find hard to grapple with and eventually nuclear weapons to deter a conventional attack from India.

Zia's course of supporting the Khalistan movement under the shadow of a covert nuclear program had left India with fewer options for a hard power recourse. The 80s saw an unsettled India that lost a prime minister to insurgency, and searching in vain for an answer to proxy warfare supported by Pakistan.

The Kashmir Phase

In the late 80s, the Punjab insurgency was reaching its endgame. India's security agencies had finally succeeded in ending a nightmare that lasted through the decade. Pakistan's attention was now moving to the exciting possibility of putting a knife into another internal fissure in India in a more familiar theatre, Kashmir. The battle of a thousand cuts was about to begin. The 1990s would create a new nightmare for India. Punjab's flames of violence, stoked by Pakistan, had not quite died down when the Kashmir fires were lit.

The Kashmir insurgency intensified in 1990. On cue, Pakistan heightened its Kashmir rhetoric. On 2 January, Pakistan's foreign minister, Yaqub Khan, came to meet his Indian counterpart, I.K. Gujral, with the usual denials about any role in promoting insurgencies in India. On

14 January, Pakistan expressed concern at the deteriorating situation in Kashmir, in what was clearly a diplomatic offensive accompanying the terror campaign unleashed in the Valley. On 19 January, the infamous Kashmiri pandit exodus from Kashmir took place, as terrorists seemed to get a free run of the Valley. Pakistani rhetoric on Kashmir was escalating to higher decibels, with frequent threats of war. In February 1990, Pakistan's newly-incubated civilian politicians, Benazir and Nawaz, were in fact competing for the shrillness of their rhetoric on Kashmir.

This was also the period when regional geopolitics was in churn, severely impacting an India preoccupied with internal woes. In June 1990, Iraq had invaded Kuwait. The Gulf war started in 1991. The Cold War had ended, and the USSR—a strong friend of India—had dissolved. America's unipolar moment was beginning. Sri Lanka was in turmoil, its ethnic battles spilling over into India. In May 1991, former PM Rajiv Gandhi was brutally assassinated by Tamil militants.

India seemed to be losing control of its internal security, even as its economy threatened to go into a tailspin, in danger of IMF default. It was in this period of external flux, accompanied by political and economic instability at home, that India encountered some of the toughest internal security challenges since independence.

Pakistan was not going to let this opportunity go by. The LeT, launched in Muridke, Punjab, in the mid-80s, sharpened its terror claws for Kashmir as it picked up steam with its training camps in eastern Afghanistan. The Kashmir-focussed terror group, Hizbul Mujahideen (HM) was formed in 1989. The destruction of the Babri Masjid in December 1992 gave a ready cause to multiple militant outfits leading to an orgy of violence, including the 1993 Mumbai blasts, engineered by the Dubai-based gangster, Dawood Ibrahim, who became a close ally of the ISI.

All-India Terror: Under the Nuclear Umbrella

When both countries went overtly nuclear in 1998, the perceived strategic parity that Pakistan attained did not live up to its promise of making military competition with India unnecessary. With Pakistan compensating for the conventional power imbalance with nuclear deterrence, this inflexion point could have served as a moment for Pakistan to abandon proxy terror as state policy. However, at the turn of the century, the opposite proved to be the case. Pakistan in fact tried terrorism under the nuclear umbrella, its nuclear assets serving as a perverse incentive to continue the low-cost policy of proxy terror. It also tried a deniable military incursion under the nuclear umbrella in Jammu and Kashmir at Kargil, only to be surprised by the military and diplomatic rebuff from India. Despite the humiliation to Pakistan's military, some sections in its security establishment saw India's strategic restraint as evidence of the success of Pakistan's deterrence.

The Kargil misadventure of 1999 was followed by the hijacking of flight IC 814 from Kathmandu, with suspected Pakistani involvement and the release of prized terrorists from India, including Masood Azhar, who went on to form the deadly *JeM* based in Pakistan. More was to come in the new century. A terror attack on the Jammu and Kashmir Legislative Assembly in March 2001 was followed by another spectacular one in New Delhi in December, with Lashkar terrorists attempting to take over India's Parliament while it was in session. This led to *Operation Parakram* on the border, with India responding angrily to Pakistan's terrorism but still not crossing the border militarily.

After 2001, Pakistan threw in its lot with the USA, when it was given a stark choice by President Bush: either you are with us or with the terrorists. However, then dictator General Musharraf fine-tuned a two-faced strategy of supporting the militant groups while appearing to side with the Americans. Soon, Pakistan faced a backlash from the terror proxies it had created. The era of 'good and bad terrorists' began, with Pakistan's forces hunting down the groups in the east that were increasingly attacking Pakistan's security forces, and protecting the 'good terrorists' who were being actively encouraged to focus their deadly talents on India.

An India-Pakistan détente was attempted by Prime Minister Vajpayee from 2003, reinforced by a visit in 2004 when Musharraf gave another solemn promise that territory under Pakistan's control would not be used against India. However, the respite from terror was brief. As Musharraf seemed to lose his grip over his country, spectacular acts of terror resumed, with the bombings in Mumbai in 2006. A painful inflexion point for India came in

Mumbai in 2008, when the trauma of a televised terror attack seared the nation. In a perplexing response, debated to this day, India still stayed its hand and refrained from taking kinetic action against the terrorists headquartered in Pakistan, although the evidence of state complicity was compelling and the national security adviser of the time had recommended such a course.

Terror under the FATF Watch

After the Mumbai attacks of 2008, Pakistan came under increased scrutiny of the FATF, a 39-member intergovernmental body combating money laundering and terrorism. The Financial Action Task Force, a Paris-based organ of the United Nations, had been set up in 1989 by the G7 to counter money laundering but added countering terrorism financing to its mandate after the 9/11 attacks of 2001. It was gradually gaining expertise in sniffing out terror financing; Pakistan was a natural port of call as the global epicentre of various terror networks.

Global trust in Pakistan plunged further in 2011, when the world's most wanted terrorist, Osama bin Laden, was killed by US Navy Seals in an army safe house deep within Pakistan. The country was placed in 2012 on the FATF 'grey list', from which it exited three years later after promising strict adherence to the UN counterterrorism regime, particularly UNSC resolution 1267 on designated terrorists. However, the leaders of militant outfits continued to be untouchables in Pakistan and brazenly appeared in public, as the country lapsed into the grey list in 2018 and risked being shifted to the black list.

Pakistan could again exit the grey list only in 2022, on the political promise to the West of future good behaviour. This was accompanied by the geopolitical assurance of assisting in Afghanistan, but with only nominal action against leaders of designated militant outfits.

Particularly from 2011, Pakistan has been facing twin blowbacks: increasingly brazen and deadly internal attacks by local terror outfits like the TTP, and a severely damaged international reputation as a state sponsor of terror. Global scrutiny made it harder for Pakistan to attempt large-scale terror. Also, the mounting pressure after 2016 of India's 'assured retaliation', added to the cost of terror operations and was thus an additional factor in limiting the terror operations below India's threshold of tolerance and confining them geographically to Jammu and Kashmir.

A Message in Uri and Balakot

The Balakot air strikes were a defining moment in India's campaign against terrorism, confirming to the adversary that the Uri surgical strikes of 2016—even if flatly denied by Pakistan—were not a one-off aberration, but signified a major policy shift by the new Indian government. The strikes also held a larger message for the terrorists, for Pakistan and for the global community: India's threshold of tolerance of terrorism was now significantly lower.

At the UN, India's diplomacy intensified with a focus on listing JeM chief Masood Azhar under the 1267 sanctions regime. However, China was protecting its 'iron brother', defiantly, putting a block on the process. Partly as a result of India's effective diplomacy, China realised that it was losing considerable diplomatic capital in defending a terrorist.

Pakistan's mainstream media had also bravely joined the chorus of teaching some common sense to its leadership. The *Dawn* argued that that the JeM was in the spotlight once again and Pakistan should act. It reminded its readers that the JeM had attacked Pakistan's President Musharraf when he had proscribed them. It nudged Pakistan to win the support of the international community by acting against them. The FATF, as also the IMF, were emerging as effective global instruments that helped modify some of Pakistan's behaviour.

Tackling Terror's Newer Avatars

While cross-border infiltration of terrorists into India has declined significantly, this relative quiet may not be a full stop, but a comma before the next attempt at a major operation. Pakistan's pause in terror seems tactical because the strategic goal is of a chronically embedded policy: to constantly challenge and destabilise India. Some in Pakistan hint that its posture of perennial hostility towards India may have changed. As evidence, they cite the fact that it refrained from exploiting the 2020 Sino-Indian standoff in eastern Ladakh and-despite that conflict, initiated and honoured the LOC ceasefire of February 2021.

Few in India would buy the theory of any change in heart in Pakistan on cross-border terrorism. For one, Pakistan's agencies are shifting their attention to newer technologies that are emerging to assist terror. Cyber warfare, fifth generation information wars and drones add newer dimensions to the terror story.

Pakistan has clearly stepped up activities against India in the domain of cyberspace. Experts report a surge in cyber-attacks against Indian computer networks and sophisticated campaigns on social media platforms. In fact, Pakistan-based hackers are hyper-active in defacing Indian websites and in attacking government networks to steal confidential data and disrupt the functioning of critical infrastructure.

Drones are the new weapons of choice. Reports suggest that in the first nine months of 2022, till September, security forces observed the illegal entry of 191 drones into Indian territory from Pakistan. Of these, 171 entered into Indian territory through the India-Pakistan border along the Punjab sector while 20 were seen in the Jammu sector. Seized UAVs were smuggling in arms and narcotics into Indian territory. Intelligence suggested that the drones also carried Afghan heroin for financing terror operations in the Valley and in Punjab, in operations predictably managed by the LeT and other ISI-backed terror outfits with camps across the border.

Clearly, when the traditional forms of support to terror are checked, newer ones emerge. Under PM Modi, India's posture of zero tolerance to terrorism has escalated costs and increased disincentives for the cross-border sponsors of terror and, India's security agencies and diplomats are successfully responding to the newer forms of this forever war.

11

WATER SECURITY IN INDIA

Bharat Lal

In the beginning of 2023, India's population crossed 1.4 billion and became the most populous country in the world. It has 17.5 per cent of the world's population but less than 4 per cent of the world's freshwater resources. More than 40 per cent of its area is arid and semi-arid with erratic and scanty rainfall leading to perpetual paucity of water, impacting the lives and livelihood in these regions. India's 70 per cent population lives in villages and more than 47 per cent people are dependent on agriculture. India is also home to the world's largest livestock population with animal husbandry contributing significantly to the rural economy. In 1947, food grain production in India was about 32 million MT, which has risen to 320 million MT in 2021. India has achieved food security and is also able to export food grains to other countries. With the growing impact of climate change, the rainfall pattern is changing and the shortage of water is visible in many parts of the country.

In India, per capita freshwater availability in 1951 was estimated to be 5,177 cubic metres, which came down to 1,508 cubic metres in 2014 and is projected to be 1,465 cubic metres in 2024. If effective action is not taken to reverse this trend, by the year 2050, per capita freshwater availability is expected to drop to 1,235 cubic metres with huge regional variations in many areas, going below 1,000 cubic metres. If per capita water availability is below 1,100 cubic metres, the area is characterized as water-stressed. In India, out of 734 districts, 256 are water-stressed. There are many regions where the ground water table is depleting.

India is changing and changing fast. Its people have become aspirational. A new aspirational middle class has emerged and expanding. People not only aspire for a better quality of life but also want enhanced ease of living so that they are able to devote time to productive work and realize their dreams. It took 60 years after Independence for India to become a one trillion US dollar economy in 2007. However, India took only another seven years to become a two trillion US dollar economy. Since 2014, with strong focus on governance, development and public service delivery, it took only five years for India to become a three trillion dollar economy in 2019. However, the COVID-19 pandemic, which started in the beginning of 2020 in Wuhan, China, impacted this growth trajectory. However, India overcame the challenges of the COVID-19 pandemic, rebound and became the fastest growing big economy in the world. As a result, India became the world's fifth largest economy and aspires to become the second largest by 2047, when it will be celebrating 100 years of its independence.

The world's most populous county and its youngest workforce with rising aspirations in an expanding and diversifying economy, has led to increasing demand of water in all sectors. While agriculture accounts for nearly four-fifth of water consumption, the industry's rising importance for the economy will take its share in total water consumption to 18 per cent by 2050 from the present 10 per cent. From an economic perspective, assured availability of water is crucial for high economic growth and prosperity. With about 33 per cent women's participation in the workforce, which was only 24 per cent in 2014, assured availability of clean tap water at homes will free women and girls from the drudgery of fetching water. This is the lowest hanging fruit, which will help in further expand the economy and raise family incomes to fulfil the goal to raise the per capita income from about 2,300 US dollars today to more than 16,000 US dollars in 2047, thus catapulting India into a middle-income country.

To ensure that this developmental journey is not interrupted, ensuring adequate water availability in every part of the country to meet the demand of every sector throughout the year is of paramount importance. A country like Israel has achieved this successfully. In India, a drought-prone Gujarat with 70 per cent area under arid and semi-arid zones has shown the way.

In the mid–1980s and late 1990s, Gujarat experienced the worst droughts of the century. Every third year used to be a drought year causing massive loss to agriculture. Central and South Gujarat receive about 80–200 cm rainfall whereas areas like North Gujarat and Kutch get less than 40 cm, leading to perpetual scarcity of water. It witnessed recurring droughts and a decreasing groundwater table that led to enormous damage to its agrarian economy and livelihood. The scarcity of water also affected the dairy industry, and paucity of water led to a loss in industrial production. It caused and pushed women to walk miles to fetch water. Every year, a few thousand tankers would be deployed as a mitigation measure to meet drinking water needs. At times, transportation of water through railway rakes became a new normal. In city after city, town after town and village after village, especially in North Gujarat, Saurashtra and Kutch, women used to wait for hours together standing in long lines with their utensils to fetch water from water tankers. The whole year, the government and district administration will keep on planning and taking emergency measures to make arrangement for water, fodder and relief work due to a prevailing drought-like situation in the state. As a result, productivity plummeted.

In 1999-2000, the Gujarat economy grew by 1.02 per cent, which went down further to minus 4.89 per cent in 2000-2001. During 1997-2002, the GSDP growth of Gujarat was only 2.8 per cent. The paucity of water not only destroyed crops but also posed a serious threat to the health of people and their livestock. Every year, cattle-rearing communities popularly known as maldharis (nomads) took their cattle away from Saurashtra and Kutch to eastern and southern parts of Gujarat and neighbouring states in search of water and fodder. The maldharis with their livestock walking on highways used to be a common sight. In a few districts and blocks of Saurashtra, outward migration of people reached such a high proportion that starting with 1971, the population in these areas started going down. Of course, the situation worsened due to a devastating earthquake on 26 January 2001 on

Republic Day with its epicentre in Kutch, leading to loss of lives and destroying livelihoods and critical infrastructure.

Gujarat needed a leadership to focus on development, accelerate economic growth and ensure ecological security. Against this backdrop, on 7 October 2001, Narendra Modi took over the responsibility of Chief Minister of Gujarat. The goal was clear—bring the state back on its feet again. For him, citizen-centric development and eco-restoration of Gujarat became the focus of governance.

During the early years of his stewardship of Gujarat as chief minister, three problems were most visible, which had a high impact—water scarcity, shrinking economy, and rehabilitation and reconstruction of earthquake-affected areas of the state. Paucity of water was the limiting factor in Gujarat's quest for faster socio-economic development and high economic growth. In his 13 years at the helm, Narendra Modi ensured water security and put the state on the path of inclusive socio-economic development and high economic growth. As a result of developmental policies and water security achieved, in the last two decades Gujarat has clocked double digit growth bringing prosperity and improved quality of life for its people.

During 1999 to 2002, more than 10,000 road tankers used to be deployed to provide drinking water to people living in North Gujarat, Saurashtra and Kutch. Even the eastern parts of Gujarat where a very large tribal population lives, was also not untouched by water scarcity. Daily two trains used to take water to Saurashtra. There used to be discussion and planning sessions for the possible evacuation of people from three towns of Saurashtra.

Known to be the dairy capital of India, Gujarat witnessed a turnaround from water scarcity to water security in the first decade of the 21st century resulting in high agricultural and economic growth. Its transformation involving environment-friendly policies, climate-resilient engineering, and strengthened grassroots leadership created a space to 'value' water in a different way. The realization that paucity of water is the limiting factor to socio-economic development and the quest for high economic growth, led to a series of policy initiatives and action to achieve long-term water security.

To find a long-term sustainable solution, water was placed at the centre of the state's developmental policy agenda and governance. The focus was to ensure adequate and assured availability of water so that lives and livelihoods are not affected adversely due to shortage of water. Focus was placed on ensuring clean drinking water to every home in every part of the state. With this clarity and firm resolve, a series of policy decisions including the integration of the water sector to manage demand and supply as well as to ensure accountability at different levels, were taken.

As the first step, completion of the over-delayed Sardar Sarovar dam was accorded the highest priority. With the realization that rainwater has to be collected and stored wherever possible, rainwater harvesting and/or artificial recharge of underground aquifers were planned using watershed principles including the use of satellite data for the identification of appropriate locations for rainwater harvesting structures, and studying the aquifer patterns for their recharge. The effort was to develop and use groundwater resources to not just meet the current need but also future uses without creating unacceptable environmental consequences. In this endeavour, people's participation was the key and effort started to make water everyone's business.

To ensure accountability at all levels, the water supply sector was re-organized in the form of three organizations to carry out specific tasks. The Gujarat Water Infrastructure Limited (GWIL), a company created to build and manage bulk-water transfer infrastructure; the Gujarat Water Supply & Sewerage Board (GWSSB) to manage the water distribution network and supply water to villages, towns, cities and industrial estates; and a unique organisation named the Water and Sanitation Management Organisation (WASMO) was created to facilitate decentralized, demand-driven, community-managed water supply systems in villages by empowering local village communities and panchayats in partnerships with civil societies, community-based organizations, SHGs, NGOs, etc. Local communities were put in control of local water sources and water supply systems.

Drought-proofing strategy was adopted by building climate-resilient infrastructures. A state-wide drinking water grid was built to provide clean water free from contaminants, by transferring surface water from a distance through bulk water pipelines of about 2,000 km and distribution network of over 1.15 lakh km along with numerous hydraulic structures, storage sumps, water filtration, and treatment plants. The canal system was expanded and strengthened to carry water from the Sardar Sarovar reservoir to drought-prone areas of the state.

To ensure water security, especially in drought-prone North Gujarat, Saurashtra and Kutch, a unique approach to transfer Narmada floodwater to these regions through a series of canal networks was taken up by constructing a 332-km long 'Sujalam Sufalam' unlined recharge canal, on the northern side, parallel to the Narmada main canal. In addition, to meet water requirements, especially in areas with salinity in groundwater, desalination plants were set up and so far, four such plants producing 270 MLD water have been taken up in coastal areas of the State.

At the village level, local committees were formed called 'Pani Samitis' as a sub-committee of the village panchayat, under the Panchayati Raj Act. Acknowledging women's role in managing water and the fact that they are disproportionately and acutely affected by its shortage, it was decided that at least half the committee would be women along with proportionate representation from the weaker sections of society. This also paved way for the industrious women of Gujarat who have already been part of self-help groups or the milk revolution, to form and lead the all-women Pani Samitis in many villages. Five women from every village were trained to test water quality. Local people especially women were trained as masons, plumbers, electricians, pump operators, motor mechanics, etc. to join the skilled workforce required to build, manage, operate and maintain water supply systems in every village of the state.

Pani Samitis were trained to undertake the responsibility of water resources management and water service delivery including collecting water user charges. WASMO introduced innovative mechanisms such as direct transfer of funds to the accounts of Pani Samitis to plan and implement various water works. WASMO provided an enabling environment to local communities to take full ownership of their in-village water supply systems. This pioneering work received global recognition in the form of the United Nations Public Service Award in 2009.

In addition, a special purpose vehicle namely, the Gujarat Green

Revolution Company, was set up to educate farmers to adopt water efficient irrigation technologies such as drip and sprinkler irrigation systems. To encourage farmers to adopt such micro-irrigation systems, it provided electricity connections on a priority basis as well as financial support. As a result, about 20 lakh hectares of farmland have been covered under micro-irrigation systems in Gujarat.

It was noticed that every year only about 24 per cent capacity of water reservoirs in North Gujarat, Saurashtra and Kutch used to get filled during the monsoon whereas water demand was highest in these regions. For optimal utilization of the existing water storage infrastructure, the 'Saurashtra Narmada Avtaran Irrigation' (SAUNI) Yojana was planned and taken up under which, every year during the monsoon, surplus water from the Narmada is transferred and stored in about 115 reservoirs of Saurashtra and neighbouring areas. This work is benefiting about 8.25 lakh acres of land in Saurashtra. Similarly, small lift irrigation schemes have been taken up in southern and eastern Gujarat where tribal communities reside, providing assured irrigation to about 3.50 lakh acres of farmland, thus improving their income. Similarly, a massive campaign was taken up to build check dams, ponds, bandhs and bori-bandhs by involving local communities, especially farmers.

The synergy of modern technological advances and traditional wisdom combined with people's participation brought out the best outcomes. Gujarat was one of those states where the ground water table was going down by 3 to 8 metres annually. These steps ensured that by 2008, depletion of the ground water table was reversed and it started rising throughout the state except in a few scattered blocks. Preserving resources for future generations and timely interventions was integral to a vision that brought Gujarat to where it is today. Every household in Gujarat has an assured supply of clean tap water, thus not only improving the quality of life and enhanced ease of living, but families now have more time at their disposal to use it gainfully. If water security can be achieved in drought-prone Gujarat, it is possible that this integrated and focused approach can be scaled up across the country.

Water Security at National Level

In India, floods are quite common in the eastern region, especially in the states of Assam and Bihar. However, drought is more pervasive in central and Western India, starting from South Haryana, Rajasthan, Madhya Pradesh and parts of Uttar Pradesh, especially Bundelkhand, Gujarat, Maharashtra, Karnataka, Telangana and Andhra Pradesh. These areas need a sound water management policy to overcome perpetual drought-like situation and scarcity of water.

It is well known that whatever water is received through rainfall and snowfall in the higher Himalayas, need to be stored for which earth surface needs to be kept clean. If land surface is contaminated with human excreta and garbage, it is next to impossible to collect and store clean water in dams, reservoirs, lakes, rivers, etc. In fact, human excreta spread on the land surface also poses the risk of contaminating underground aquifers. The link between sanitation and water is so strong that Narendra Modi, in his first term as the prime minister, focussed on eliminating the age-old practice of defecation in the open. On 15 August 2014, in his first Independence Day address to the nation, he launched the 'Swachh Bharat Mission' (Clean India Mission), which is the world's largest behavioural change programme to make India 'Open Defecation Free'. As a result, after five years of its launch, on the 150th anniversary of Mahatma Gandhi's birth, that is, 2 October 2019, all villages in the country declared themselves open defecation free. To sustain the open-defecation free status of villages and make water bodies contaminant free, Swachh Bharat Mission 2.0 was also started with the focus on reducing waste production and its collection, treatment, reuse or safe disposal. The key impact areas of this mission are bio-degradable solid waste management, grey water management, plastic waste management, and faecal sludge management (FSM).

Following the success of an integrated water management approach in Gujarat, in 2019, after getting re-elected for the second term, Prime Minister Narendra Modi created a single unified ministry to handle all matters related to water and the Ministry of Jal Shakti was formed by merging the Ministry of Water Resources, River Development and Ganga Rejuvenation, and the Ministry of Drinking Water and Sanitation. This reorganization brought much-needed synergy in working and put in place a lot many agencies, institutions, and autonomous bodies to work together on various water-related issues in an integrated manner.

To make water everyone's business and encourage people to focus on rainwater harvesting and artificial recharge of aquifers, in 2019, the 'Jal Shakti Abhiyan' was launched as a mission-mode initiative especially in 256 water-stressed districts of the country. Under the Jal Shakti Abhiyan, extensive awareness activities and convergence of efforts and resources were mobilized to build rainwater harvesting and recharge structures to achieve source sustainability. The scale of ambition is gauged by the fact that the prime minister termed it as a 'Jan Andolan'—a people's movement that targets major silos of water conservation and rainwater harvesting, rejuvenation of water bodies, watershed development and reforestation.

Jal Jeevan Mission and Other Judicious Interventions

On 15 August 2019, Prime Minister Narendra Modi announced the Jal Jeevan Mission (JJM) to provide tap water to every rural household in the country by 2024. At the time of announcement, out of 19.36 crore rural households, only 3.23 crore (16.72%) households had tap water connections. After country-wide consultations to firm up implementation strategy and processes, implementation on the ground started on 25 December 2019, that is, on Good Governance Day. The motto of the mission is building partnerships, working together, changing lives. In the last three years, despite the COVID-19 pandemic, the Jal Jeevan Mission has been implemented with speed and scale. In the planning and implementation, all stakeholders, that is, state governments and their para-statal organizations, rural local bodies/panchayats, NGOs, reputed institutions, etc., have been involved. Under the Jal Jeevan Mission, one of the largest mobilizations has taken place. The approach has been to ensure that no one is left out, which is in consonance with the prime minister's motto of Sabka Saath, Sabka Vishwas, Sabka Prayas. As a result, by January, 2023, more than 11 crore (57%) households have provision of clean tap water in their households. All households in more than 1.53 lakh villages and 123 districts have become Har Ghar Jal, that is, every household has assured clean tap water supply.

Similarly, provision of tap water in more than 86 per cent schools and 82 per cent anganwadi centres have been made along with tap water in toilets and hand washing facilities for children, thus ensuring better health and development of children.

The Rs. 3.60 lakh crore Jal Jeevan Mission uses data analytics and AI in planning, implementing and monitoring. Each tap water connection to a household is authenticated by the Aadhaar number of the head of the family. Under JJM, service delivery in terms of quality, quantity, regularity and pressure in pipelines as well as ground water table is to be monitored through sensor-based IoT solutions for which large scale pilots have been completed successfully, thus ensuring accountability, transparency and assured service delivery, which is at the heart of good governance.

To ensure that water supply systems are planned, implemented, monitored, operated and maintained by local communities, 10–15-members Pani Samitis/Village Water & Sanitation Committees (VWSCs) are being set up across the 6.5 lakh villages of the country. In these Pani Samitis, a minimum 50 per cent are women members and 25 per cent representation is from the weaker sections of society. These Pani Samitis, which are a sub-committee of the village panchayat, are being empowered to adopt an end-to-end approach involving the four key components, namely, water resource management source sustainability, water supply, operation and maintenance, and grey water treatment and re-use. Local youth are being upskilled to work as masons, plumbers, electricians, motor mechanics, fitters, pump operators, etc., to ensure availability of trained human resources in villages to carry out routine operations and maintenance. Paucity of drinking water affects the lives of women and girls most and therefore concerted efforts have been made to make sure that they are truly empowered. Thus, five women in each village are being trained to use field test kits (FTKs) to test the quality of the water supplied, conduct sanitary surveys, and upload the data on the JJM Management Information System. Such skilled resources at the local level are expected to help in disaster risk reduction and mitigation measures, as well as build local resilience.

Furthering the cause of 'making water everyone's business', 185 organizations including UN agencies, trusts, foundations, and others, have been roped in as sector partners to dovetail their resources and efforts to accomplish the goal of 'Har Ghar Jal'. Massive capacity building, training, and community mobilization initiatives are being undertaken to build capacity, refocus, and train public health engineers, village representatives, and Pani Samiti members, for which 104 key resource centres (KRCs) have been engaged as partners. States are also enlisting the help of more than 14,000 local NGOs, VOs, CBOs, women's SHGs, and other organisations as implementation support agencies (ISAs) to assist GPs/VWSCs in realizing the vision of building local public utilities.

To enhance the capacity of public health engineers through learning opportunities, at the national level, the Dr. Shyama Prasad Mukherjee National Institute of Water and Sanitation (SPM–NIWAS) has been set up at Kolkata as an apex institution for public health engineering (PHE) in the water, sanitation and hygiene (WASH) sector. The institute, adopting a 'hub-and-spoke model', will partner with key resource centres (KRCs), centres of excellence (CoE) and professor chairs being set up across the country and work in areas of training and capacity building, education, research and innovation, and outreach and consulting, with a special focus on ensuring source, financial and environmental sustainability.

Marking India's stronghold in the global digital era and leveraging the technological potential within the country, innovative technologies are being promoted. A 'Technical Committee' chaired by the Principal Scientific Advisor (PSA) to the Government of India, comprising state representatives, scientists, innovators, and others, has been formed to utilize emerging technology and deliver novel solutions. Sensor-based IoT pilots for smart measurement and monitoring of the daily water supply are underway in more than 100 villages, which are being scaled up throughout the country. These sensor–based ioT systems have been developed within the country in partnership with the Ministry of Electronics and Information Technology (MEITY) and C-DAC. Similarly, portable water quality testing devices have been developed in partnership with Start-Up India by creating an ecosystem for all stakeholders.

Digital governance is being promoted to ensure transparency, accountability, effective fund utilization, and assured service delivery through several measures such as the publicly available Jal Jeevan Mission dashboard that provides progress updates in a user-friendly and captivating manner. A dedicated water quality management information system (WQMIS) has also been put in place showing results of water quality tests and enabling the public with information at their fingertips.

The Jal Jeevan mission has brought a new awareness of public health and assured supply of clean tap water to every home. A recent study by Nobel Laureate Prof Kramer, University of Chicago, showed that with only 50 per cent coverage with provision of potable tap water supply, JJM is able save the lives of at least 1.36 lakh children every year from water-borne diseases. In the last three years, water-borne diseases have come down significantly.

Ensuring Groundwater Security

India's dependence on groundwater is very high. Groundwater plays a significant role in influencing decentralized, demand-driven, and community-managed water supply systems where local communities, especially women, are engaged in intelligent water management for long-term water security in villages. In today's climate-risk world, especially this decade where more rain is predicted in fewer days and the patterns gets erratic year after year, it is crucial more than ever to speed up the work to collect and store rainwater, use it judiciously and make the most thorough treatment and re-use. The Government of India, over the last eight years, has taken multiple initiatives to popularise the circular economy of water in the spirit of people-driven systems. Ensuring efficient water governance to make the country water-secure, the government called for active and judicious interventions at multiple levels to address every single element of water management.

The Atal Bhujal Yojana is one such programme that is scaling up community-led sustainable groundwater management. It is a pioneering experiment involving the empowerment of local communities, facilitating their participation and ownership, with the support of local stakeholders to ensure groundwater security. The Pradhan Mantri Krishi Sinchayee Yojana, another programme to enhance water-use efficiency, focuses on micro-irrigation encouraging farmers to adopt water-saving technologies. Post

COVID-19, in 2021, the Jal Shakti Abhiyan was expanded throughout the country as the 'catch the rain where it falls' campaign.

Water security, water conservation, and water-use efficiency have become the priority to ensure long-term sustainability. Convergence of efforts and resources under schemes like the Jal Jeevan Mission, MGNREGS, Atal Bhujal Yojana, Pradhan Mantri Krishi Sinchayee Yojana, 15th Finance Commission-tied grants to rural local bodies for water and sanitation, etc., has provided huge opportunities to dovetail resources at the village level offering optimal utilization of funds and ensuring financial sustainability.

Namami Gange, another major initiative started in 2015, is a programme to revive and revitalize the holy river, Ganga, the cradle of Indian civilization. The programme is geared to restore the wholesomeness of the river and maintain its geo-hydrological and ecological integrity. The programme strives to maintain water security in the entire Ganga Basin, with policies and programmes on demand side management, floodplain protection, conservation of wetlands and springs, improving groundwater through aquifer recharge, re-use and recycle, and improving water use efficiency. Namami Gange has emerged as a model to restore other river systems. Now 13 other major rivers have been taken up for making them perennial and pollution-free. These rivers give sustenance to people by ensuring food and water security.

Among other programmes, the National Aquifer Mapping Programme is the world's biggest programme of its kind. It envisages the formulation of aquifer management plans to facilitate sustainable development of groundwater. The Pradhan Mantri Krishi Sinchayee Yojana (PMKSY), which aims to complete long-pending irrigation projects, is being implemented with the vision of ensuring 'Har Khet ko Pani' (water for every field) and improving water-use efficiency as encapsulated in the idea of 'More Crop, Per Drop'. The inter-basin transfer of water and interlinking of rivers have been given a new direction so that not only floods are managed but flood water is made available to drought-prone regions of the country.

Way Forward

Local communities have been placed at the centre of water governance. As discussed above, gram panchayats and/or its sub-committees, that is, village water and sanitation committees or Pani samitis, are envisaged to plan, implement and manage local water supply systems under Jal Jeevan Mission. It has put women in the leadership role and has ensured that at least half of the members in the village water and sanitation committees/Pani samitis are women. Considering that they are the worst sufferers of the despicable practice of open defecation, it is only natural that they should lead the effort against it. In the irrigation sector also, participatory irrigation management (PIM) has been promoted. With the formation of a new in the form of the Ministry of Cooperation, the agriculture sector and cooperation is getting a direction.

It is often said that management and the use of modern technology have been missing in the water sector. The path shown by Gujarat and under implementation throughout the country is showing the way forward to achieve water security. Centred around people, technology and sustainability, these initiatives have paved the way for affordable, scalable, and reliable models for the entire world, especially the global South. Various initiatives taken in the water sector have taken the shape of a silent revolution bringing prosperity to the last person at the bottom of the pyramid.

Ensuring water security for the success of the nation's growth and prosperity is the way forward. The progress has so far been exemplary. However, the issues of climate change would throw up new challenges, high intensity erratic rainfalls being one of the many. This essentially means that efficient water management will remain a work in progress in which correct institutional and functional mechanisms will ensure success. The well-begun journey to achieve water security needs to be taken forward with renewed vigour and commitment so ensure that socio-economic development and high economic growth ushers in prosperity.

12

Attracting Global Investment: A New India in the Making

Nalin Kohli

Over the past eight years, India has witnessed developments that reflect major improvement in the lives of its citizens. Industry, business reforms, and infrastructure development has fuelled the economy. Technology and innovation, start ups and enterprise, health, education, agriculture and trade—all have received significant impetus. India's global standing has never been stronger. Since 2014, Narendra Modi as Prime Minister, has pursued in mission mode, an agenda to transform India at an unprecedented speed and scale. This agenda of holistic transformation is laying the foundations for India to emerge as an economic superpower, the target for which is 2047. It is the year when India will achieve one hundred years of independence and what the Modi government calls *Amrit Kaal.*

Today, India is the fastest-growing large economy in the world. After 75 years of democracy since its birth as an independent nation in 1947, India is now the world's fifth largest economy with a GDP of USD 3.5 trillion. It has grown a 100 times than what it was seven decades ago.

The Modi government is actively making India an attractive destination for investments. The launch of 'Make in India' in 2014 has more than doubled the annual FDI during this period. It has grown from USD 35 billion to USD 84 billion in a decade. The thrust of business reforms has yielded good results. Corporate tax has been reduced drastically to 22 per cent for existing units and 15 per cent for new units, which is amongst the lowest globally. Under the Production-Linked Incentives (PLI) Scheme, financial incentives exceeding USD 26 billion have boosted domestic production in 14 sectors. Under the Business Reform Action Plan (BRAP) over 300 reforms across 72 action points for state governments to develop an investor-friendly ecosystem, have been introduced. The introduction of the Goods and Services Tax and an Insolvency and Bankruptcy Code has led to tremendous change. Simultaneously, over a thousand redundant laws and thousands of unnecessary compliance burdens have been done away with. Additionally, a one-stop digital platform for all investor approvals across the central and state governments are helping draw further investments. Such reforms have enabled India to impressively scale the World Bank's Ease of Doing Business Ranking to jump 79 positions in five years from 142 to 63 in the rankings

Digital India has received a keen thrust under Prime Minister Modi to make economic benefits more inclusive. Nearly 1.3 billion people have a unique digital identity under the Aadhar regime. Over 1.2 billion people have mobile phones and 750 million own smart phones. The introduction of the United Payments Interface (UPI) has been a stupendous success with 74 billion transactions taking place in the calendar year 2022 itself. By linking the Aadhar number with a mobile number and a creation of about 480 million bank accounts, the government has successfully saved billions of dollars by transferring benefits of government schemes directly to targeted beneficiaries. Over 30 million houses have been built for the poorest of the poor and 90 million women have benefited from free gas connections. Sanitation has been in focus. Nearly 110 million toilets have been built, particularly in rural areas. An estimated 3.2 million people received free treatment under the Ayushman Bharat central government scheme. Almost USD 200 million has been disbursed as loans for micro entrepreneurs. India also is the only country which prints every currency note in Braille.

Even as several major economies are still reeling under the impact of the COVID-19 pandemic, India witnessed a V-shaped recovery with its GDP contracting 24 per cent in the first quarter of the year before bouncing back impressively by 20 per cent in the fourth quarter of the same year. This economic recovery was on account of the Atmanirbhar Bharat effort as also a strategic response in fighting the disease through the largest vaccination program in the world. A phenomenal 2.2 billion vaccine doses were administered via Cowin, the national digital vaccine registration platform.

A good indicator of a thriving economy is the purchasing power of the general public. India's per capita income has grown from about USD 1,000 to about USD 2,300. It is estimated that people in India are now earning much more than what they did in 2014.

The Modi government recognises that small is beautiful and has extended support to smaller-sized enterprises. Under the Atmanirbhar Bharat Abhiyan, credit support has been provided to eligible micro, small and medium enterprises (MSMEs) to meet their operational liabilities. The start up ecosystem launched in 2016 in India has flourished. Today, India is the world's third-largest start up ecosystem with 107 Unicorns and 80,000 plus recognised start ups. India contributes to one out of every 10 unicorns globally.

Infrastruture development has received tremendous attention. The PM Gati Shakti, a national master plan for multi-modal connectivity, is a GIS-based technology platform to improve multimodal connectivity, logistics efficiency and ensure seamless movement of goods and services. This master plan has the potential of saving over billions of dollars annually by improving logistics efficiency.

Since 2014, the total length of national highways has increased from 91,287 km to 140,937 km, with an average 25-km per day road construction, up three times from the previous government's pace of development. The flagship Sagarmala Programme envisions the promotion of port-led development in the country by harnessing India's long coastline and waterways for domestic and international maritime trading. The aviation sector has also grown under a comprehensive National Civil Aviation Policy where, for the first time since independence, the focus is on making flying more affordable and convenient. Under the UDAN scheme connecting smaller towns, 425 new routes have been introduced and over 10 million citizens have taken to the skies, quite literally. The number of operational airports has doubled from 74 to 140 since 2014, with a plan to further develop and operationalise 220 airports over the next five years.

Narendra Modi, as India's Prime Minister, is putting in place the building blocks required to achieve a 25-year roadmap for India at 100. The vision is to make India the world's second-largest economy at USD 32 trillion, increase the per capita income 10 times to USD 20,000 and grow exports 12 times to USD 8 trillion. India's *Amrit Kaal* is a reality in the making.

[Source: Invest India Factbook 2023 and similar material.]

13

Anchoring Security in the Region: India's Vision and Initiatives

Maj Gen Dhruv C. Katoch

Viewed for long as a continental power, a major foreign policy initiative of India, effectively articulated by Prime Minister Modi since coming to power in 2014, was reclaiming India's heritage as a maritime nation. Speaking on 12 March 2015 at the commissioning of the Barracuda ship built by India and presented to the National Coast Guard of Mauritius, Prime Minister Modi spoke of India's maritime heritage and seafaring tradition dating back to the time when Lothal port in Gujarat was built. This was perhaps one of the earliest sea ports in the world. The Indian Prime Minister also laid down his vision for the Indian Ocean Region. This encompassed working towards a safe, secure and stable Indian Ocean Region that delivers prosperity to all—the SAGAR vision, SAGAR being an acronym for Security And Growth for All in the Region.[1]

On 01 June 2018, while speaking at the Shangri La Dialogue in Singapore,[2] Shri Narendra Modi once again highlighted India's past as a seafaring nation. He spoke of the oceans and Varuna—the Lord of all Waters—mentioned in the Vedas and Puranas, tracing India's maritime linkages to those ancient times. He also referred to Indian texts which defined

India with reference to the seas—the land lying between the Himalayas to the north and the oceans in the south—stating that India's destiny has, since ages, been shaped by the Indian Ocean which even now, holds the key to India's future. The continuous reference to India's past as a seafaring nation has to be seen in the context of India's vision for the region. Here, the Prime Minister defined India's area of interest as stretching from the east coast of Africa to the west coast of America, encompassing the entire Indo-Pacific region and all the littoral countries therein. The destiny of the world, he said, will be deeply influenced by the course of developments in the Indo-Pacific region, and despite legacy challenges, can be shaped in our 'collective hopes and aspirations'. Towards this end, the vision that Narendra Modi propounded was for a free, open, and inclusive region, embracing every nation in a common pursuit of progress and prosperity. He called for a common rule-based order for the region, where the sovereignty and territorial integrity of all nations, regardless of their size or strength, is respected. He spoke of equal access to the use of common spaces, both on sea and air, for freedom of navigation and unimpeded commerce and reiterated India's commitment to support free and open navigation and a rule-based order in the Indo-Pacific.

The vision laid down is not mere grandstanding, but based on India's increasing expanding sense of its role in international affairs. In October 2015, Shri Manohar Parrikar, India's then Defence Minister, released a document on India's revised maritime military strategy titled 'Ensuring Secure Seas: Indian Maritime Security Strategy' (IMSS-2015). Net security as a concept was defined in this document as "...the state of actual security available in an area, upon balancing prevailing threats, inherent risks and rising challenges in the maritime environment, against the ability to monitor, contain and counter all of these".[3] In 2009, the then US Defence Secretary, Mr. Robert Gates, in his address at the Shangri La Dialogue-2009, said, "...We look to India to be a partner and net provider of security in the Indian Ocean and beyond...".[4] What exactly is implied by the term 'net security provider? It is as of now an ambiguous term, open to different interpretations. However, the idea that India can be a net security provider to the region has its roots both in India's geographical location as well as in her capability to undertake such a role. India's former Prime Minister,

Dr. Manmohan Singh, also spoke of India being well placed to become a net security provider to the region, in an address he gave at the foundation stone-laying ceremony of the Indian National Defence University (INDU), Gurugram.[5] The statement was more in the nature of a possible future intent, rather than being policy driven, which was why we saw no movement towards that end. In a lecture delivered in January 2016, Mr. Shiv Shankar Menon, who was the National Security Advisor to Prime Minister Manmohan Singh, stated that India has been inhibited by limited capabilities in taking up such a role as also the fact that other states were providers of security. However, with both these limiting factors now undergoing a change, India would have to make "real political and military contributions to stability and security in this region that is so critical to our economy and security".[6]

Since 2014, India has moved slowly yet steadily in taking up this role. India has provided assistance to countries struck by natural disasters and evacuated personnel from friendly countries along with her own personnel from war zones. The Indian Navy, by patrolling the waterways, has also acted as a deterrent to piracy in the Indian Ocean. India is now not seen as just a provider of net security in the region, but its role is increasingly being accepted as such by many of the littoral countries in the IOR, as seen in the recent statement of the Sri Lankan High Commissioner to India, Shri Milind Moragoda. In an interview, he said, "Very clearly, India is the anchor when it comes to security in this region, on that there is no issue. As the security guarantor of the region, India is the anchor."[7] Such statements have become routine from foreign diplomats. The USA too has been looking forward to becoming a responsible power to share the security burden, and they have sought India's role in providing the same in the region. While earlier there was a certain level of circumspection in taking such a step, India's foreign policy has been far more assertive since 2014 with respect to building relations with its immediate neighbourhood as well as in the wider Indo-Pacific region and beyond. India's foreign and economic policy is now also bolder in looking after India's interests, overcoming the hesitancies of yesteryears.

India as a Provider of Net Security

Anchoring security in the region and being a net provider of security has multiple implications. Broadly, it pertains to addressing common security concerns in the region such as dealing with terrorism, piracy and natural disasters such as earthquakes and tsunamis, as also concerted action to deal with the consequences of climate change. There is both a military and diplomatic component to deal with such issues. The former involves capacity building, joint training, protocols for providing military aid and deployment of military forces to stabilise a situation. On the diplomatic front, it encompasses building bilateral and multilateral partnerships to deal with issues of concern.

In June 2014, just a month after taking over as the Prime Minister of India, Narendra Modi gave directions to the Indian Space Research Organisation (ISRO) to develop a satellite for use by all the member-countries of the South Asian Association for Regional Cooperation (SAARC). Within three years, India launched GSAT-09, a communication satellite, which now provides, tele-communication, tele-education, and a host of other services to the beneficiary countries, and also provides data on weather, alerts on natural disasters and the like. At that time, Prime Minister Modi stated that such a satellite would be useful for the development of all SAARC nations, with India playing a key role in the initiative. However, as Pakistan backed out of the initiative, the satellite was named South Asian Satellite.[8] This was not merely an exercise in optics. It signalled a change in India's outreach to its immediate neighbourhood and was in line with the new Neighbourhood First Policy of India. This had, in its ambit, a diverse range of topics to include cooperation in the economic sphere, as also in the fields of technology, education, connectivity through digital, surface transport and air transport, energy, and environment and climate change. Neighbourhood First also leveraged existing multilateral arrangements such as the Bay of Bengal Initiative for Multi-Sectoral Technical and Economic Cooperation (BIMSTEC). This grouping is useful in bringing together member-countries on a common platform, which could not be done in SAARC due to the intransigent attitude of Pakistan. Similarly, as Pakistan opposed the regional motor vehicles agreement at a summit in Nepal in 2014, Bangladesh, Bhutan, India and Nepal made a separate agreement, the Bangladesh, Bhutan, India and Nepal (BBIN) Motor Vehicles Agreement (MVA), to facilitate seamless flow of passenger, personal and cargo vehicular traffic between and among the BBIN countries. The Neighbourhood First policy complements both

India's Act East Policy which focuses on the ASEAN countries as well as the Look West Policy, which focuses on West Asia. The impetus given to all these initiatives has helped in building strong relations between India and her neighbours stretching from Singapore to the Gulf.

Beyond the region, India plays a major role in BRICS and the SCO. BRICS is an acronym for five major emerging market economies—Brazil, Russia, India, China and South Africa. While the initial formulation was to act in concert on economic issues, the ambit was widened later to encompass political and social issues. Formed in 2006, the first summit was held in 2009. India hosted the eighth and thirteenth BRICS summits in 2016 and 2021, respectively. In 2016, the focus was on counter-terrorism, economies and climate change. The 2021 Summit was held through video conferencing due to the pandemic. In terms of GDP, China, India, Brazil and Russia currently rank 2nd, 5th, 8th and 11th, respectively in world rankings and South Africa ranks at 32nd place.[9] China, India, Brazil and Russia are also part of the G20. It is important to note that the BRICS countries, within themselves, account for about 42 per cent of the global population.[10]

The Shanghai Cooperation Organisation (SCO)—a political, economic and security organisation—was formed in 2001 as a successor to the Shanghai Five, a mutual security grouping of five countries, China, Kazakhstan, Kyrgyzstan, Russia and Tajikistan, formed in 1996. India was admitted as a full member in June 2017. Security remains the primary concern of the SCO, with the main threats being described as terrorism, separatism and extremism. Member-states also cooperate in the military field by holding joint exercises. Economic and cultural cooperation also forms part of the agenda. India's presence in the SCO is not inconsequential. It provides India a forum to deepen its relations with the Central Asian Republics as well as a forum to further anti-terrorism efforts in the region.

India's membership of the BRICS and SCO also gives it influence in the Eurasian heartland. However, being part of these groupings does not indicate alignment with either Russia or China. However, these organisations remain an important forum to look at regional and global challenges and enhance cooperation to address common goals and objectives. In 2023, New Delhi will hold the presidency of the SCO.

India is also a member of the Quadrilateral Security Dialogue, popularly called the Quad—a four-nation grouping of Australia, India, Japan and the USA. Formed in 2007 under the initiative of Japanese premier, Shinzo Abe, its seeds were sown three years earlier post the tsunami of 2004, which saw India, Australia, Japan and the USA work together on disaster response. However, the Quad failed to take off and remained dormant for the next ten years, till it was again revived by Abe in 2017. In the 2017 ASEAN Summit in Manila, the leaders of the four countries, Prime Minister Abe of Japan, Prime Minister Modi of India, President Trump of the USA and Prime Minister Turnbull of Australia, agreed to revive the Quad to counter Chinese aggressiveness in the Indo-Pacific region. China was dismissive of the Quad gathering, the Chinese foreign minister describing it as "a headline grabbing idea," and scoffing, "They are like the sea foam in the Pacific or Indian Ocean: they get some attention but will soon dissipate."[11] However, that dismissiveness no longer exists and Chinese leaders now express deep concern about the Quad. In March 2021, the joint statement issued at the Quad Summit spoke of a shared vision for a free, open, inclusive and resilient Indo-Pacific, and to promoting a rule-based order, rooted in international law.[12] China now describes the Quad as the most consequential challenge to Chinese ambitions in the Indo-Pacific.

It was Modi's push to the Quad in 2020, following the clash in Galwan between Indian and Chinese soldiers, which left 20 Indian soldiers dead that led to the Quad re-assessing its strategic priorities and expressing the intent to take on Chinese aggressiveness in the Indo-Pacific. Mike Pompeo, the US Secretary of State, was blunt in stating that it was Washington's goal to both institutionalise the Quad as well as to build a true security framework for the region to counter Chinese aggressiveness. India invited Australia to join the Malabar exercise held in the Indian Ocean in November 2020 and for the first time, all the Quad members took part in it.[13]

For India, the Quad represents a totally different set of groupings than both the BRICS and the SCO. The former has a focus on India's interests in the Eurasian heartland, while the Quad is aligned to India's concerns in the Indo-Pacific, with a focus on free and open navigation, which is vital for India's security and economic growth. What stands out today is the clear enunciation of India's national interests, which India is no longer hesitant to state and pursue. This marks a shift from the erstwhile policy of non-alignment to one of strategic autonomy. India will no longer kowtow to one of the power blocs. Its size and its stature make India a pole in its own right and this is the new vision that Modi has enunciated.

Capability and Political Will

However, mere intent is not adequate to provide the region that element of assurance that India can be a net security provider to the region. There must also be exhibited capability and political will. Both these aspects have been on display over the last eight years through HADR (Humanitarian Assistance and Disaster Relief) operations. Such operations have been particularly effective in power projection in a benign manner.

When the Maldives faced a water crisis in December 2014, it was India which responded by sending 1,200 tons of drinking water by ship and air to the beleaguered island.[14] Then, on 25 April 2015, when a 7.6 magnitude earthquake struck Nepal, Prime Minister Modi immediately reached out to his counterpart in Nepal and offered India's assistance.[15] The earthquake caused death and destruction on an unprecedented scale, with 9,000 deaths, over a lakh injured and about 8 million people impacted. Beside huge financial and material aid, India also deployed its National Disaster Relief Force (NDRF) to assist in relief and rescue efforts, the same being termed Operation Maitri.[16] Thereafter, in August, PM Modi asserted India's commitment to the reconstruction work in Nepal after the devastation caused by the earthquake.[17] In 2017, it was again India that assisted the governments of Bangladesh and Sri Lanka in dealing with a devastating cyclone and flood, respectively.[18] Most such crises occur in the oceanic belt between the Red Sea and the Malacca Strait. India, by her unique geographical location, is uniquely placed to provide assistance to countries impacted by natural disasters.

The proactive nature of India's foreign policy was also witnessed in the evacuation of Indian personnel from Yemen in 2015, where war raged between Houthi rebels and the Yemen government supported by Saudi Arabia. Not only did India evacuate all her nationals but also evacuated nationals from

26 countries who sought India's help.[19] This commitment of India to bring back her nationals wherever they may be when they are stranded due to war or natural calamities has now become a hallmark of India's foreign policy. We saw this in Operation Vande Bharat, launched on 7 May 2020, to bring back Indians from all across the globe, stranded due to COVID-19. In 2021, in Operation Devi Shakti, the Indian Armed Forces carried out the evacuation of hundreds of Indians stranded in Afghanistan after the collapse of the government and takeover of Afghanistan by the Taliban.[20] This feat was repeated in war-torn Ukraine, when Russian forces attacked Ukraine on 24 February 2022. Over the next fortnight, over 16,000 Indians had been evacuated from Ukraine and the remnants that remained were evacuated shortly thereafter. The rescue mission, codenamed Operation Ganga, was a testament to India's growing influence, especially as many big countries were facing difficulty in doing so.[21] A total of 147 foreign nationals were also evacuated in Operation Ganga.[22] All this has added to India's credibility and reliability, which has, in a sense, made India an anchor in the region for providing assistance in times of need.

Capacity Development

Soft power has impact only if it is backed by both economic and military capability. In India, it was the Narendra Modi government since 2014 that has given a concerted push to empowering the people at the grass roots level which has had an impact on the masses. As stated by Finance Minister Nirmala Sitharaman during the release of the 100th edition of Economic Newsletter of the BJP in Karnataka on 14 August 2022, the government's approach has been to empower individuals, not through entitlement but by extending the reach of welfare schemes to all. The premise was that every citizen has a right to basic facilities.[23] It is this focus of the government that has prevented a backlash experienced by most of the world due to the COVID-19 pandemic and the war in Ukraine. Of particular importance was the focus on financial inclusion, which took shape through the Jan Dhan Yojana, and which enabled millions of citizens to open bank accounts. By linking these accounts to the Aadhar card, and by creating extensive telecom access to all services, it was possible to transfer subsidies directly to beneficiaries through their mobile phones. This by itself is a revolution that has seamlessly taken place across the country, which has promoted the use of digital technology for financial transactions, even at the lowest level.

The emphasis on indigenous production has also now become a buzzword in Indian industry, with the corporate sector focused on achieving laid down goals and reducing dependence on imported goods. No surprise then that India is now poised to become a three trillion dollar economy and has recently overtaken the United Kingdom to become the fifth largest economy in the world.[24]

In the military domain, great progress has been made to enhance capability. The purchase by India of the C130J Super Hercules aircraft greatly increased the strategic lift capability of the Indian Air Force (IAF). While six aircraft were purchased in 2011, a further six were ordered in 2017 which has doubled the IAF's strategic lift capability. Along with this, in September 2015, India signed a deal with the USA for 22 Apache and 15 Chinook helicopters. The former is an attack helicopter which has greatly augmented Indian strike capability and the latter is a transport helicopter providing strategic lift capability and is especially useful in the mountains. India also signed a deal for six additional Apaches in 2020.[25] To further augment air capability, India signed a deal with France for the purchase of 36 Rafale multi-role fighter jets in fly-away condition, in September 2016. The last batch of three aircraft arrived in India in February 2022.[26] This has greatly enhanced India's air capability and has shored up the depleting IAF fighter squadrons somewhat.

With respect to the Indian Navy, the launch on 2 September 2022 of India's indigenously built aircraft carrier, INS *Vikrant*, was indeed, as the tweet from the Indian Navy indicated, a momentous day for India. India has now joined a select group of countries with this capability.[27] More than anything else, it represents in a sense the coming of age of India's ship-building capability. India has already built submarines and warships and now, with the indigenous aircraft carrier, it heralds a step up in Indian ship-building capability. The Indian Army has also enhanced its capability and there is now a larger component of indigenous equipment in its armoury ranging from bulletproof vests, artillery guns, small arms, ammunition, missiles and armoured vehicles.

It is evident that India's defence sector will soon come of age, especially with the Modi government taking the initiative and giving policy directions for enhancing the role of the private sector in defence production. Since then, the corporate sector has made steady progress in enhancing India's defence capability. The defence sector will be further energised when the two defence industrial zones, one in Tamil Nadu and the other in Uttar Pradesh, become fully operational. This will pave the way for making a strong defence industrial base for India. The decision by the government to relax norms for exports as seen by the export of the Brahmos missile to the Philippines, has set the stage for India to become, in the years to come, a major defence exporter. This will further enhance India's ability to look after both its own security interests as well as that of the region.

The direction which the Modi government has given to its foreign policy has enabled a more pragmatic approach in dealing with the near and far abroad, always keeping the centrality of India's core interests at heart. Within the country, policy initiatives have created a climate of inclusiveness and a spirit of entrepreneurship which has fuelled the Atmanirbhar mission, making India the fastest growing large economy, despite turbulent times across the world. All this has inspired confidence in the world community in the Indian growth story, which in turn has made India an acceptable anchor for stability and a net security provider in the region. This also fits in well with India's cultural heritage, and its larger message from ancient times that the World is one Family (*Vasudhaiva Kutumbakam*). It is the Modi government which has propagated this thought and has set about to achieve it in full measure. By being the security anchor in the region, India can look after her own interests as well as those of its neighbours. India under Modi is well poised for this role.

Endnotes

1. Text of Prime Minister Modi's remarks on the commissioning of Coast Ship *Barracuda* is available at https://pib.gov.in/newsite/printrelease.aspx?relid=116881
2. The full text of Prime Minister Modi's address is available at https://www.mea.gov.in/Speeches-Statements.htm?dtl/29943 Prime+Ministers+Keynote+Address+at+ Shangri+ La+ Dialogue+ June+01+2018
3. Indian Maritime Security Strategy (IMSS-2015). p. 80.
4. https://www.rsis.edu.sg/wp-content/uploads/2014/09/PB_140903_India-Net-Security.pdf

5. https://www.thehindu.com/news/national/india-well-positioned-to-become-a-net-provider-of-security-manmohan-singh/article4742337.ece
6. Shiv Shankar Menon; "We Must Now Choose"; lecture on "India's Changing Geopolitical Environment" at the 'Changing Asia' series of Lectures, New Delhi, 23 January 2016, available at http://www.outlookindia.com/article/we-must-now-choose/296484
7. https://www.hindustantimes.com/india-news/india-is-anchor-of-regional-security-says-sri-lanka-s-envoy-milinda-moragoda-101661953409971.html
8. https://www.business-standard.com/article/current-affairs/how-the-south-asia-satellite-will-help-india-boost-ties-with-neighbours-117050100356_1.html
9. https://www.worldometers.info/gdp/gdp-by-country/
10. https://brics2021.gov.in
11. https://www.foreignaffairs.com/articles/united-states/2021-08-06/why-quad-alarms-china
12. https://mea.gov.in/bilateral-documents.htm?dtl/34318/Joint+Statement+ from+ Quad+Leaders
13. https://www.minister.defence.gov.au/media-releases/2020-11-03/australia-joins-exercise-malabar-2020
14. https://economictimes.indiatimes.com/news/international/world-news/maldives-water-crisis-india-sends-1200-tonnes-of-fresh-water/articleshow/45397733.cms
15. https://www.indiatvnews.com/politics/national/pm-modi-speaks-to-nepal-president-after-earthquake-28681.html
16. https://ndrf.gov.in/operations/nepal-earthquake-apr-2015
17. https://www.newindianexpress.com/nation/2016/aug/20/India-committed-to-Nepals-post-quake-reconstruction-PM-Modi-1511251.html
18. https://thediplomat.com/2017/06/indias-projection-of-power-through-humanitarian-assistance-and-disaster-relief/
19. https://www.thehindu.com/specials/the-great-yemen-escape-operation-rahat-by-numbers/article7089422.ece
20. https://www.outlookindia.com/national/operation-ganga-to-vande-bharat-india-s-biggest-evacuation-missions-in-recent-past—news-184730
21. https://www.thehindu.com/news/national/2135-indians-brought-back-by-11-special-flights-says-ministry/article65199046.ece
22. https://www.opindia.com/2022/03/147-foreign-nationals-from-18-countries-evacuated-under-operation-ganga-kiev-kharkiv-most-challenging/
23. https://www.hindustantimes.com/india-news/focus-of-modi-govt-s-growth-model-is-to-empower-poor-sitharaman-101660413785467.html
24. https://www.worldometers.info/gdp/gdp-by-country/
25. https://swarajyamag.com/news-brief/india-negotiating-purchase-of-more-apache-attack-and-chinook-heavy-lift-helicopters-senior-boeing-official
26. https://www.thehindu.com/news/national/france-has-delivered-all-36-rafale-jets-to-india-french-envoy/article65643887.ece
27. https://www.indiatoday.in/india/story/ins-vikrant-commission-india-first-indigenous-aircraft-carrier-pm-modi-kochi-live-updates-1995473-2022-09-02

14

Resolving Challenges and Management of Water Resources in India

Uttam Kumar Sinha

Introduction

The challenges of water, both in terms of availability and distribution, are not easy to comprehend. Lack of information, awareness and unreliable water data add to the complexity. US President John F. Kennedy, acknowledging the complexities of water had said that the person who can solve the world's water problems should receive two Nobel Prizes—one for peace and the other for science. Talking about political leaders, Indira Gandhi, the prime minister of India, did not care much about water *per se* or the water professionals who she felt unnecessarily hyped the issue. For her, water was a 'means to an end'. The end mattered more, whether it was economic growth, poverty alleviation, employment, etc.

Over the past many decades, the world has witnessed several water themes such as 'Go with the flow' suggesting the natural rhythm of rivers and water flow and minimum intervention; 'Water is what you make of it' implying that water can be a great peace builder as much as a catalyst for conflict and if not conflict, certainly disputes.

There is now a greater understanding of the theme on the nexus of water with food and energy. Likewise, resource management has also evolved from 'water management' to 'water resources management' to 'integrated water resources management'. While the knowledge curve on water has certainly risen, policies yet seem to be struggling to keep pace. The unknown dimensions of water, whether from the socio-political perspective or the economic and the ecological, make it a wicked resource. Often searching for water solutions leads to many more problems. Understanding the nature of water is, therefore, critical—whether from the perspective of demand-supply or from a conflict-cooperation frame, or even relating water to the system of laws.

Value of Water

There is an adage that says that you do not know the true worth of water till the wells run dry. The dependence on fresh water, particularly for irrigation, is high. Groundwater for irrigation and drinking is growing rapidly. Globally, groundwater accounts for about 50 per cent of pumping for drinking water, and 20 per cent for irrigation. In India, 80 per cent of agricultural production depends on groundwater and in the arid and semi-arid zones, 60 per cent of the water used for irrigation comes from groundwater.[1] Knowledge of groundwater resources is not exact. For example, are aquifers determined by political boundaries? What exactly are their renewal flows and their stocks? What impact does groundwater have on surface water (river flows, precipitation infiltration, groundwater pollution, etc.)? Importantly, how fast do they replenish?

Water has limited availability, which is unevenly distributed. As global economic activity and development continues, increase in water demand will be compounded by the decreasing availability of water resources in most major hydraulic basins, either because of deterioration in quality or quantity. Competition for both surface and groundwater becomes an additional factor of social and political instability, both internally and regionally.

India's Water Reserves

India probably uses more water than any other country. Several studies and reports indicate that the overall water demand for India, without major reform and investment, may be twice the available supply by 2030.[2] More specifically, the demand for water in the business-as-usual scenario will increase by 22 per cent by 2025 and 32 per cent by 2050,[3] which will require the use of all available water resources in the country. In terms of per capita water availability, the decline has been sharp—from over 5,000 cubic metres (m^3) per year in 1947 to 1,544 m^3 in 2011.[4] India is already in the water stress category (below 1,700 m^3 per year).[5] India's 20 major river basins, according to various studies, are below the water scarcity threshold of 1,000 m^3 per year. Large populations in different parts of India are already experiencing water scarcity and even absolute scarcity. It is estimated that about 700 million people will face various levels of water challenges ranging from the extreme to moderate by 2030.

Various studies conclude that by 2030, water demand in India will be principally driven by population growth and the domestic need for food, in particular, rice, wheat and sugar. Clearly, the drivers of water challenges are principally tied to development and economic growth with the agriculture sector being the largest water withdrawer. The interplay of food, energy and water (FEW) within the complex context of population increase, rising standards of living and resource constraints poses interlocking challenges to sustainable environmental policies.

Constitutional and Legal Perspective

The legal framework of water in India is diverse and seeped in its history and culture. It draws elements from ancient local customs and traditions; during colonial times, laws on irrigation were framed. International conventions, as mentioned earlier, such as the Helsinki Rules and the 1997 UN Convention, also strengthen water laws. Principles and norms of 'equitable share' and 'no significant harm' help in dealing with inter-provincial disputes. Discourses such as 'water as a human right' and maintaining the 'environmental flow' has equally influenced water laws in India.

While water is recognized in the Constitution, both in terms of 'basic need and a right', it must be emphasised that such recognition has evolved through judicial interpretation. Constitutionally, water is a state subject (Entry 17 in the State List). However, there is also Entry 56 in the Union List providing "Regulation and development of inter-State rivers and river valleys to the extent to which such regulation and development under the control of the Union are declared by Parliament by law to be expedient in the public interest." The entries refer to specific uses of water in terms of water supply and irrigation. Since the emphasis on irrigation facilities is predominant canals, embankments, storages and drainage, show a heavy influence of engineering and technocratic points of view.

Central intervention comes in when there is an inter-provincial water dispute. The provisions (Entry 56 in the Union List) are clearly laid out in the Rivers Board Act (1956) and the Inter-State River Water Disputes Act (1956). The latter empowers the Centre to set up tribunals to adjudicate disputes over water sharing. The Centre can also intervene in the interests of protecting the environment or for developing a water basin "expedient in the public interest" by enacting a law to give the Union the legislative power over the river. No law till date has been passed to bring any river under the Union.

Apart from the two entries, as mentioned above, Article 262 and the Inter-State Water Disputes Act, 1956, enacted under it look at water disputes which largely relate to irrigation. Water has thus been divided in the constitutional scheme with the Centre and the State having the power to legislate over various aspects and demonstrating in the process the separation of power. Placing water as a state subject was part of the federal exercise to deepen and widen democracy.

As India unravels the water challenges, the laws will have to equally evolve. An integrated water resource management will require an integrated water law, a more comprehensive one especially in terms of ecology and rivers and water bodies as 'living entities'. The classical interpretation of water as a private property has moved considerably to being a common pool resource.

There has emerged recently the debate whether water should be put in the Concurrent List and whether by doing so would mean centralization. It prises the old debate on whether the constitutional provisions over water need to be relooked. Some earlier commissions, particularly the Sarkaria Commission, constituted to look at Centre-State relations, have not favoured any changes. In times of coalition politics that emphasise decentralization and federalism, shifting water to the Concurrent List would be politically incorrect if not a retrograde step. A number of water experts strongly recommend that the enabling provisions of Entry 56 should be fully utilized and the Rivers Board Act are activated.[6] There is also an argument, more recent, that major rivers of India should be a national asset or national natural resource.

There has been considerable development on the aspect of human right to water and water rights. However, both are legally and conceptually different. First, though not incorporated explicitly in the Constitution, there is a fundamental right to water for every person in India that has been judicially evolved over the years. For example, 'Right to life' under Article 21 has been interpreted as an entitlement for 'pollution free' and 'safe drinking' water for every person. The closest that the law makers have come to incorporating the right to water as a fundamental right was when the National Commission in 2002 recommended that a new Article 30D be inserted in the Constitution. It has yet to be enacted.[7] The fundamental right to water may not be forever elusive. After all, the right to education of a child from 6-14 years of age was also judicially evolved and eventually became a fundamental right under Article 21A.

Second, the Constitutional space relevant for water rights and management is expressed through parts IX and IXA of the 73rd and 74th Amendments that came into effect in 1993. The two amendments brought in local self-governance as an enforceable ideal and obliges states to create local bodies to "function as institutions of self-government" in rural and urban areas. The panchayats, as institutions of self-governance, were given power and authority and subjects like drinking water, water management and even minor irrigation and watershed development came under their jurisdiction. In the urban areas, municipalities were given similar powers of self-governance looking after matters like water supply for domestic, industrial and commercial purposes. The 73rd and 74th amendments led to what is described as "inspired changes" in the panchayats, municipal corporation and municipal council laws leading to responsibility and accountability in the services provided, particularly water.

What about the rights of rivers? Rivers are the visible part of the water stock of a country along with fresh water lakes, ponds, swamps and marshes. Rivers are shared in the Indian subcontinent and there is a transboundary nature to it. This will be explained later. Wide-ranging legislations have been attempted for the conservation of rivers. In order to cleanse itself, rivers must flow. A river must equally have space for accommodating floods and the floodplains must be recognised as a natural system of rivers. Rivers are a part of the larger ecosystem and are a mediated resource. The protection of the ecosystem therefore becomes important. In March 2017, the Uttarakhand High Court ruled that the Ganga and Yamuna, the Gangotri and Yamunotri glaciers, along with other related natural elements are "legal persons" with all corresponding rights, duties and liabilities of a living person. This was, however, overruled by the Supreme Court a few months later arguing that it was "legally unsustainable".

The first question, therefore, that comes up is whether water is a state subject? It is broadly true. However, it requires a nuanced understanding. In fact, water, as explained, is both in the State and Union lists. There is a potential role of the Centre in relation to inter-state rivers, both in terms of dispute and development provided parliament legislates on this, which it has under the River Board Act (RBA) 1956. Should we now change the constitutional structure and shift water to the Concurrent List? There will be intense political debate over such a move to give more power to the Centre and thereby disturb the fine constitutional balance. As Ramaswamy Iyer often argued, "The point here is, and I think this is very important, is that when you place water or rivers in the constitutional debate the tendency is to look at it from a federalist argument or centre-state relations and really not from a water perspective." Not surprisingly, the RBA has remained a dead letter. Parliament has not brought any river under its purview because of political ramifications. States have been wary about River Basin Organisation and the Centre's role. Issues of dominance over centralisation and bureaucratization often impede a workable centre-state relationship. Keeping in mind the political difficulties in placing water in the Concurrent List, the more rational approach would be for the Centre to exercise entry 56 and activate the river board through the principles of consultation, dialogue and understanding.

National Water Policies

As explained earlier, Entry 17 and Entry 56, Article 262 and the Inter-State Water Disputes Act 1956 have all contributed to the federal approach to water. Bolstering all this is the inclusion of water management in the list of functions to be devolved to panchayats and nagarpalikas according to the 73rd and 74th Amendments and Schedules 11 and 12. There are other federalist features like the Central Groundwater Authority set up in 1997 and the Central Water (Prevention and Control of Pollution) Act, 1974. India has also had the National Water Policy since 1987, which was revised and updated in 2002 and 2012. In fact, India is one of the first developing countries to have a NWP along with Mexico. The current government is working on a new water policy which would be the third in a span of 25 years.

One could argue about the necessity for another document, given that the last water policy has yet to be fully implemented. Be that as it may, states have lagged behind in implementing the earlier provisions. A new water policy has to seriously reflect on the inadequacies of implementation. The basic principles of planning, development and management of water resources are adequately explained in the 2012 NWP. One cannot fault the document for not factoring an integrated approach that adheres to the local, national and regional contexts. Equity and social justice is also outlined in approaches to water development. It essentially comes down to implementation and poor coordination between the Centre and the states. One notable aspect of the 2012 document was the "economic principles to guide the pricing of water." The ground reality has been radically different. No state, in the federal system, has the will or the inclination to charge for irrigation water. This is equally true when it comes to pricing of electricity for pumping water. It is now an appropriate time to examine whether the NWP has had any perceptible impact on improving water management practices in the country, and, if not, why.

India has a range of water data reports. In 1999, a comprehensive document titled "Integrated Water Resource Development: A Plan for Action", was published by the Ministry of Water Resources. It provided a comprehensive summary of data, problems and policies. One of the latest documents on water is from the Prime Minister's Council on Climate Change, of June 2008 entitled, "National Action Plan of Climate Change (NAPCC)". It envisages eight national missions of which the National Water Mission is central to the action plan. It states:

> *A National Water Mission will be mounted to ensure integrated water resources management helping to conserve water, minimise wastage and ensure more equitable distribution both across and within states. The Mission will take into account the provisions of the National Water Policy and develop a framework to optimize water uses and increasing water use efficiency by 20 per cent through regulatory mechanisms and differential entitlements and pricing.*

The national water document based on new understanding and knowledge and a unified national perspective is the National Water Policy 2012. It relooks, reconsiders and candidly observes some of the earlier water approaches and management practices. For example, it says:

> *With a growing population and rising needs of a fast developing nation as well as the given indications of the impact of climate change, availability of utilizable water will be under further strain in future with the possibility of deepening water conflicts among different user groups.*[8]

It further says:

> *Low consciousness about the scarcity of water and its life sustaining and economic value results in its mismanagement, wastage, and inefficient use, as also pollution and reduction of flows below minimum ecological needs. In addition, there are inequities in distribution and lack of a unified perspective in planning, management and use of water resources.*[9]

Significantly, it states that internal water management cannot be delinked from external water approaches:

> *Inter-regional, inter-State, intra-State, as also inter-sectoral disputes in sharing of water, strain relationships and hamper the optimal utilization of water through scientific planning on basin/sub-basin basis.*[10]

More recent has been the Draft National Water Framework Bill, 2016, proposed as model legislation and to be adopted by states through a broad national consensus. Although India has a low per capita water consumption;

it lags behind in the efficient use of water across sectors. Continued population growth and the impact of global warming along with inadequate conservation and huge wastage are putting enormous pressure on water resources. The various revised documents suggest that India's policy exercise on water issues is trying to respond to ground realities.

The Central and state governments, despite the inherent difficulties in the federal structure, have endeavoured to develop the water resources within the constitutional framework. The efforts, however, have not kept pace with the rise in demand for water. The absence of a strategic vision for one and lack of trust between centre and state for another has added to the water woes. With challenges like climate change, India needs a better response and implementation mechanism in dealing with the management of water resources. Structural reforms in the water sector focusing on deficit and surplus management has to be planned and implemented within the federal framework, whether it is creating new data systems or institutional restructuring or river basin planning.

Comprehensive Understanding of Water

Over the last half or more decade, possibly one of the most modernizing policy approaches of the Narendra Modi government has been to prioritize water. Water is indispensable to governance and development plans, livelihood and healthy life, expressed as *Sujalam sufalam* (water for prosperity) and the Swachh Bharat Abhiyan. It is also a key instrument of regional prosperity and integration. It is not surprising that many of the Modi's government big-ticket programmes like Swachh Bharat Mission, Swachh Bharat Urban, Swachh Bharat Gramin, Namami Gange Programme, Smart Cities Mission and Inland Navigation are centred on the indispensability of water. That apart, India is committed to the Sustainable Development Goals (SDGs). The 17 SDGs guide countries as they aim to eradicate extreme poverty, reduce inequalities and effectively deal with climate change by 2030. Many of the goals (SDG-2, SDG-3, SDG-7, SDG-13, SDG-15, SDG-16 and SDG-17) are centred on water, sanitation and hygiene, proving again the centrality of water. One of the objectives of SDG-6, in particular, is to 'expand international cooperation and capacity-building support to developing countries in water and sanitation-related activities and programmes.'

While water has undoubtedly emerged as an issue of great concern and urgency, but with the multiplying demand on it, the availability of which remains constant, water hardship is impending. The robust and comprehensive water policy of the Modi government will take into account the rapidly changing water conditions in terms of quality, quantity, and the uneven distribution of water. The role of enforcement and monitoring agencies like the EIA (Environment Impact Assessment) will be effectively enforced. The purposeful participation of civil society will be equally crucial for greater awareness and balance of development and water resources.

Much of the past policies on water were narrowly framed on the principle of 'water management' that entails manipulation of water for specific uses through water-based projects. Clearly, the more comprehensive policy of PM Modi for protection, development, and utilization of water resources, including surface and underground water, is being developed. This hydrological shift to a more rational and integrated 'water resource management' that treats water bodies as one hydrological unit embracing the 'conjunctive use' of both surface and underground water resources and their sustainable development will act as a positive catalyst for national development and integration.

ENDNOTES

1. *Water, a shared responsibility*. The United Nations World Water Development Report 2, Paris, UNESCO Publishing, 2006, p. 128.
2. National Workshop on Integrated Water Resources Management, Central Water Commission, Government of India, 2015, p. 2.
3. International Water Management Institute, India's Water Future to 2025-2050: Business-As-Usual Scenario and Deviations, Research Report 123, 2007.
4. Central Water Commission, Water and Related Statistics, 2015.
5. Water Stress 1000-1700 m^3; Water Scarcity 500-1000 m^3; Absolute Water Scarcity Below 500 m^3. See Water Scarcity Clock, World Data Lab.https://worldwater.io/about.php
6. Ramawamy R. Iyer, "Should water be moved to Concurrent List?" *The Hindu* (New Delhi), 18 June 2011.
7. Videh Upadhaya. "Water Rights and the 'New' Water Laws in India". India Infrastructure Report, 2011, pp. 57-58.
8. Draft National Water Policy (2012) as Recommended by National Water Board in its 14th meeting held on 7 June 2012 See http://mowr.gov.in/writereaddata/linkimages/DraftNWP2012_English9353289094.pdf
9. Ibid.
10. Ibid.

15

PM's Galloping Steps to Make India Vishwa Guru

Sanjay Tandon

It was an epic moment for India when it assumed the mantle of the presidency of the G20 adding a new feather in the cap of Prime Minister Narendra Modi, who has been working assiduously for regaining the international prestige of India.

Saluting the Indian Prime Minister, French President Emmanuel Macron expressed confidence in India taking over the presidency of the powerful G20 and said that "Prime Minister Narendra Modi would bring everyone together to build a peaceful and a sustainable world".

US President Joe Biden described India as a strong partner of the USA and said he was looking forward to supporting his "friend" Prime Minister Modi during India's G20 presidency.

Sharing a picture of himself and Prime Minister Modi in a tweet, Macron endorsed the theme of "One Earth, One Family, One Future" that India has chosen to work on during its presidency of the G20.

Dynamic Foreign Policy

In 2014, when Narendra Modi was elected the prime minister of the world's largest democracy, the world watched in expectation as to what his foreign policy would be. He has brought a new vigour to India's foreign policy, strengthening and renewing ties with old friends, while making new friends across the globe.

For example, he has strengthened India's ties with Israel, France, the United Kingdom, Japan, the United States of America, and South Korea, and also initiated and built relationships in West Asia (Iran, Saudi Arabia, Israel) and with New Zealand and Australia.

PM Narendra Modi has struck a fine balance of continuing relations as well as cultivating fresh ties, which will prove strategically significant in the medium and long-term. The 21st century will be characterized by proactive, ambitious and innovative diplomacy with the underlying theme of 'India First'.

Path-breaking 'Make in India' Initiative

One of the first initiatives that the Prime Minister undertook soon after assuming office was to launch the 'Make in India' campaign to facilitate investment, foster innovation, enhance skill development, protect intellectual property and build the best in manufacturing infrastructure.

These exercises resulted in a road map for the single largest manufacturing initiative undertaken by a nation in recent history. They also demonstrated the transformational power of public-private partnership, and have become a hallmark of the 'Make in India' program. This collaborative model has also been successfully extended to include India's global partners.

'Make in India' has identified 25 sectors in manufacturing, infrastructure and service activities and detailed information is being shared through interactive web portals and professionally-developed brochures. FDI has been opened up in defence production, construction and railway infrastructure in a big way.

The obsolete and obstructive frameworks of the past were dismantled and replaced with a transparent and user-friendly system that is helping drive investment, foster innovation, develop skills, protect IP and build state-of-the-art manufacturing infrastructure. The most striking indicator of progress is the unprecedented opening up of key sectors including railways, defence, insurance and medical devices, to dramatically high levels of foreign direct investment.

Swachh Bharat Abhiyan

"A clean India would be the best tribute India could pay to Mahatma Gandhi on his 150 birth anniversary in 2019," said Shri Narendra Modi when he launched the Swachh Bharat Mission at Rajpath in New Delhi on 2 October 2014.

The Swachh Bharat Abhiyan is the most significant cleanliness campaign by the Government of India. Shri Narendra Modi led a cleanliness pledge at India Gate, in which about thirty lakh government employees across the country joined. He also flagged off a walkathon at Rajpath and surprised people by joining in not just for a token few steps, but marching with the participants for a long distance.

The Swachh Bharat Abhiyan has become a 'Jan Andolan' receiving tremendous support from the people. Citizens too have turned out in large numbers and pledged for a neat and cleaner India. Taking the broom to sweep the streets, cleaning up garbage, focussing on sanitation and maintaining a hygienic environment have become a practice after the launch of the Swachh Bharat Abhiyan.

People from different sections of society have come forward and joined this mass movement of cleanliness. From government officials to jawans, Bollywood actors to sportspersons, industrialists to spiritual leaders, all have lined up for this noble work. Millions of people across the country have been day after day joining the cleanliness initiatives of government departments, NGOs and local community centres to make and keep India clean.

Pradhan Mantri Jan Dhan Yojana

The Pradhan Mantri Jan Dhan Yojana (PMJDY), one of the biggest financial inclusion initiatives in the world. It was announced by Prime Minister

Narendra Modi on 15 August 2014 from the ramparts of Red Fort. While launching the programme on 28 August, the Prime Minister had described the occasion as a festival to celebrate the liberation of the poor from a vicious cycle.

The scheme ensures access to a range of financial services like availability of basic savings bank accounts, access to need-based credit, remittances facility, insurance and pension

Against the original target of opening bank accounts of 7.5 crore uncovered households in the country by 26 January 2015, banks have already opened 12.54 crore accounts as on 31 January 2015 after conducting a survey of 21.06 crore households with deposits exceeding Rs. 10,000 crore. The target was set after conducting a survey of 21.02 crore households in the country. Today, coverage of almost 100 per cent has been achieved. Out of the accounts opened, 60 per cent are in rural areas and 40 per cent are in urban areas. The share of female account holders is about 51 per cent.

The Pradhan Mantri Jan Dhan Yojana provides a platform for universal access to banking facilities with at least one basic banking account for every household, financial literacy, and access to credit, insurance and pension facility.

The PMJDY has the objective of financial inclusion for all by providing basic banking accounts with a debit card with inbuilt accident insurance. The main features of the PMJDY include Rs. 5,000 overdraft facility for Aadhaar-linked accounts

The Pradhan Mantri Jan Dhan Yojana not only serves as an important example of governance in the mission mode but also demonstrates what a government can achieve if it is committed to the welfare of the people.

Ayushman Bharat

Yet another initiative of the prime minister that has played a pivotal role in transforming the health services in the country is the National Health Protection Scheme also named as the Äyushman Bharat scheme under which five lakh medical insurances have been completed so far.

Those covered under the scheme come from the lower income groups and it provides cover to about 50 crore people.

The Modi government has ensured an allocation of Rs. 10,000 crore in its budgets every year.

Exemplary Fight during COVID

The prime minister has always been an inspiration for the entire nation for the Antyodaya campaign which is meant to benefit the last man in the queue.

He took exemplary measures when the nation was in the grip of the pandemic. Making sure that the morale of the nation did not falter, he immediately got down to the task of ensuring that vaccination was ready as early as possible and was distributed all over the country to every nook and corner.

Not just that, India became one of the largest exporters of vaccination to help sufferers in other parts of the world.

Prime Minister Narendra Modi lauded the collective efforts of all the states in the spirit of cooperative federalism as the force that helped India emerge from the COVID-19 pandemic. India has sent a powerful message to the developing nations of the world that it is possible to overcome challenges with resilience despite resource limitations.

In order to overcome the crisis, the Centre released an economic stimulus package of Rs. 20 lakh crore under the Atma Nirbhar Bharat campaign which included many schemes like the Pradhan Mantri Garib Kalyan Yojana.

During the lockdown, the Modi government ensured the care of poor families and daily wagers. Some of the relief measures taken by the government included:

- 500 each to 19.86 crore women Jan Dhan account holders.
- LPG cylinders to be provided to 8 crore poor families for the next three months free of cost.
- 1,000 for senior citizens to tide over difficulties during the next three months.

- 28,256 crore were disbursed through PMGKY to nearly 32 crore beneficiaries.
- 50,000 crore in the Garib Kalyan Rojgar Abhiyan for returning migrant workers.

Buoyant Economy

The Prime Minister did not buckle under the pressure of the economic crisis in the COVID period and instead made sure that the Indian economy remained buoyant enough even at a time when other countries were waging a big struggle.

It is due to the Prime Minister's diligent efforts that India has emerged as the fifth largest economy in the world and is expected to overtake countries like Japan and Germany to become the third largest economy by 2027.

India has maintained a seven per cent growth rate because it has become a "bright spot" in South Asia at a time when other countries in the region are embroiled in internal conflicts and contradictions.

The Prime Minister recently delivered a very pertinent message to the nation saying that "We are on a journey to achieve an India that not only fulfils the aspirations of the people, but also stands proudly on the world stage. The people of India have great expectations for progress and improvement in governance through their participation. In the course of this transformation, while some changes are anticipated and planned, many are a consequence of market forces and larger global shifts. The evolution and maturing of our institutions and polity also entail a diminished role of centralised planning, which itself needs to be redefined.

16

India's Neighbourhood Policies: The Successes and the Challenges of the Modi Era

Maroof Raza

Introduction

Even though most of the headlines are hogged by India's relations with the USA, which has been steadily becoming stronger with every passing year as a result of the deft handling of India's diplomatic initiatives under the guidelines of Prime Minister Narendra Modi, India has finally arrived on the world stage as an eminent player in geo-politics. It had been said for many years that India was punching well below its strategic weight in world affairs, but now a variety of reasons and circumstances have put India in a unique league, whether as a member of the US-led QUAD grouping in the Indo-Pacific region, or the more recent I2U2 initiative in West Asia, and the recent rotating presidencies of the G-20 and the SCO groups. Despite considerable US and Western pressure, India has held firm to its stand to engage with Russia during its Ukraine campaign for perfectly valid strategic reasons, making it clear that India will have its independent foreign policy as in the past, and even appear to some as a 'swing state'.

However, it is the challenges of India's neighbourhood that continues to place demands on Indian diplomacy, despite the many positive initiatives of India under Mr. Modi's leadership, which have been quite considerable, even despite his outreach to India's neighbours when compared with his predecessors, especially Dr. Manmohan Singh, who could not get himself to visit any country in India's neighbourhood! On the other hand, Mr. Modi has, from the very beginning when he first took charge as prime minister of India in 2014, gave a clear message at his swearing-in ceremony, that to him, 'India's immediate neighbourhood mattered', when he invited leaders of all South Asia for a mini-SAARC summit for his swearing-in.

There is however the increasing shadow of China over the region, and there are some hardy perennials to crack like the deep-rooted anti-India narratives in Pakistan and the Chinese investments that have a strong bearing on the choices that countries like Nepal, Myanmar and Sri Lanka make vis-a-vis India. Even Bangladesh, with whom India has steadily strengthened its ties, wants much more Indian investments to counter China's footprints in that country from energy projects to highways following Beijing's announcement of a $ 26 billion total of investments in 2016, after it announced $ 46 billion for Pakistan in 2015 and $ 22 billion in India. However, there is a big gap between what China promises and what it delivers and the 'debt trap' China puts countries into, as Sri Lankans discovered in 2022. Even then, the China factor is a major diplomatic challenge for India, as Mr. Modi's government has to choose between projects in India, as against countering the Chinese footprints in the neighbourhood, as part of China's BRI (Belt and Road Initiatives), that India has openly opposed, as its flagship project, the China-Pakistan Economic Corridor, runs across the northern parts of Pakistan-Occupied Kashmir.

Nevertheless, in keeping with that spirit of his neighbourhood centric, in recent years, Mr. Modi had, at the launch of an ISRO satellite, offered to share the benefits of such initiatives with a SAARC-centric satellite for tele-medical aid, e-learning and communication with India's SAARC immediate neighbours. A similar spirit has led a growing Indian Technical and Economic Cooperation programme. The most recent was India's admirable efforts to help its neighbours and even the Western world with its COVID vaccine supplies. India's 'vaccine diplomacy' drew praise from across the world, whereas the anti-COVID vaccines that China produced had few takers. One reason in fact for the latest Chinese pandemic in 2022-23, has been the inefficacy of Chinese vaccines. Figures show that India has effectively vaccinated over 950 million citizens, a number twice as much as the rest of the world while supplying vaccines also across all continents.

However, it is territorial disputes that remain a challenge and a distraction vis-à-vis China. What was however an earlier rivalry based on economic factors, has now turned into a geo-strategic rivalry after the military standoff in the Himalayan heights following China's military intrusions in eastern Ladakh from April 2020. This had put an end to many years of effort that were invested to achieve a 'bullet-less border' arrangement. Beijing chose to abandon it for its 'expansionist' agenda. One reason for this Chinese hostility is that Beijing sees India as a spoiler to its plans to attain hegemony over Asia, even as it opens itself up to the possibilities of a conflict with Taiwan, to emulate Russia's example in Ukraine, to add to its ambitious agenda of dominance over Asia, in keeping with the Communist Party's 'Vision for 2050'. As a consequence, it may draw the USA and Japan into a conflict over Taiwan. The other possibility is of China attempting an expansion in Ladakh or Arunachal, where the USA or Japan may not intervene. It is for that possibility that India must remain prepared.

Also, for India, a matter of equally great concern is the China-Pak nexus, which poses a clear two-front threat on India's borders with Pakistan almost a vassal state enjoying Chinese supplies of fighter jets and submarines, among other things, even though the USA gave it vast supplies of major weapon systems under the pretext of America's questionable military alliance with Pakistan, after the 9/11 attacks. China apart, India's best effort to isolate Pakistan as the 'epicentre' of terrorism, has had to deal with the support Pakistan enjoys from some countries in the Gulf region, allegedly, as Pakistan assures them that its nuclear arsenal could be a suitable counter to Iran or Israel. In return, Pakistan has been repeatedly bailed out by these countries for its perennial financial mess.

However, a major achievement of Mr. Modi has been to adopt a tough, no-nonsense approach to Pakistan's sponsorship of cross-border terror attacks in India. Two examples stand out. One was the commando raids by Indian troops that followed the attack by terrorists sent from Pakistan across the LoC into Uri in J&K. This led to scores of Indian soldiers being killed in an attack. Modi gave a free hand to the Indian Army to retaliate. The commando raid that followed by India's special forces in 2016 across a heavily-mined LoC pinpointed Pakistan army-led camps in Pakistan occupied Kashmir, stunned the Pakistan army and put to rest their belief that their nuclear umbrella gave them a cover perpetually for mischief. After that, a suicide bomber's terror strike on a CRPF police convoy at Pulwama on a highway to the Kashmir Valley that killed 40-odd policemen led to a retaliatory precision Indian air strike on a Pakistani camp at Balakot beyond POK that stunned everyone, especially the Pakistani armed forces. These two attacks had put an end to Pakistan's use of nuclear threats to give a cover to their cross-border terror attacks on Indian soil. Clearly, Mr. Modi has altered the earlier narrative that India would go this further and not beyond, what Pakistan believed could escalate into a war!

India's Initiatives in the Gulf Region

No doubt India has to balance its concern about the support that Pakistan enjoys from its friends in the Gulf with India's own requirements such as oil and gas to feed India's growing energy demands, the protection of jobs that more than 8 million Indians enjoy in the Gulf region allowing them to repatriate over $ 50 billion or more to aid the Indian economy. Mr. Modi's government, in keeping with past policies, has thus formulated a policy by which India could get what it wants from the West Asian Gulf countries—primarily much of India's oil and gas supplies, as also job opportunities for its large population of skilled workers of over 8 million in that region. This has maintained the repatriation of funds back into India—about $ 50 billion in foreign exchange annually. It is this strategic requirement that Mr. Modi has rightly chosen not to ignore and his special relationships with the Kingdom of Saudi Arabia, the UAE and Oman are cases in point. He has managed to engage them without marginalizing Israel, a country that he had a special relationship with even before he became prime minister and without ignoring the issue of Palestine. A tricky tightrope walk, but executed deftly.

The fact that Pakistan continues to work hard to keep India outside the OIC conference and use them to rally support for its (hopeless) initiatives to malign India's policies in Kashmir, has been ignored by Delhi, as India's engagement with the Islamic countries has been on a bilateral basis with each of the nations, including Iran, with which the Gulf countries have their own concerns about. Kashmir apart, what the Gulf countries do watch very carefully is the political situation within India and its impact on India's large Muslim population. This remains a constant challenge for Mr. Modi's government as it has to balance the assertions of right-wing groups with a 'majoritarian' agenda within India, and how to curtail their actions, which can lead to communal flare ups and a bad press for India.

An objective assessment would lead us to conclude that while India's image as a tolerant society was questioned in the West, this has not been openly so in the Middle East, where Mr. Modi's deft diplomacy in projecting his image and that of his party is still the best choice for overseas nations to engage with and has won him many of the highest awards in Gulf countries and promises of investments. The region plays a vital role in India's economy as it supplies nearly two-thirds of India's total oil imports. Bilateral trade is also flourishing in recent years, particularly with the UAE and other Gulf states. Over the years, millions of Indians mostly from the working class have migrated to the Gulf looking for jobs and they account for a sizable share in the total remittances into India received from abroad. A less talked about factor is the concern within India's security agencies over the steady rise in influence of Islamic fundamentalists within India, based on the push of Wahabi-Salafi Islamists largely based out of Saudi Arabia, a key element in India's West Asia (Middle East) policies.

India's Act East Policy

This is another area where a big push was given by Mr. Modi to India's relations with countries in South East Asia. It first drew interest in the time of Prime Minister Narasimha Rao (in 1992), as India's 'Look East Policy' but Mr Modi scaled it to India's 'Act East Policy', making it clear that India would strive to increase trade and connectivity with that region substantially. In due course, Vietnam emerged as a rather important partner. It also allowed India to further enhance its ties with Japan, a country that has originally assisted with the growth of the region before China moved in. With Beijing's plans to dominate the sea lanes of the South China Sea and then with its Belt and Road Initiatives, both of which are far from popular in the region, there are countries keen for India to enhance its presence even as Beijing and some of its friends are not too enthusiastic about a pro-active Indian role in South East Asia. With Indian naval ships now operating therein (with an Indian naval base in Indonesia) and although India's EEZ does not extend into that region, it is now clear that India is willing to challenge the Chinese on the high-seas as it has done in the Himalayas.

From the very beginning, the Narendra Modi-led government made it amply clear that India would focus more and more on improving relations with ASEAN and other East Asian countries as per India's 'Look East Policy' which was formulated in the 1990s for better economic engagement with its eastern neighbours. However, successive Indian governments later successfully turned it into a tool for forging strategic partnership and security cooperation with countries in that region in general and Vietnam and Japan in particular. It was during her visit to Vietnam (Hanoi) that India's then foreign minister in Mr. Modi's earlier government, Sushma Swaraj, had stressed on the need for an "Act East Policy" that she said should replace India's over two decades old "Look East Policy" emphasizing a more proactive role for India in this region. This has now seen many bilateral initiatives between India and the countries of this region, but it is still a policy in the works, and not quite as fine-tuned as India's diplomats have been able to carve in the Gulf.

Indian Ocean Outreach

Connecting India's strategic space from the Gulf region to the South China Sea is the vast Indian Ocean Region (IOR), which was earlier considered India's nautical backyard, but is now steadily turning into a hotspot thanks to growing Chinese strategic presence over the region's numerous strategically located archipelagos. China's growing naval might is being used as part of China's 'Maritime Silk Road' by using ports in Myanmar, Sri Lanka, Pakistan and Djibouti, where its navy has established bases for military and trade purposes. As a counter, the Government of India started to reach out to India's maritime neighbours in the IOR with proposals of enhanced economic and security cooperation. This had begun to unfold during a visit by the Sri

Lankan President to New Delhi in early February 2015. After that, Mr. Modi embarked on a three-nation tour (*yatra)* to Mauritius, Seychelles and Sri Lanka, leaving out the Maldives (due to the political turmoil in that country then, that led to the cancellation of his scheduled visit). It was an initiative undertaken by Mr. Modi ahead of a scheduled visit to Beijing in May 2015, as New Delhi wanted to project that it commanded strategic supremacy over the IOR and that its relations with its maritime neighbours had a cordial tenor as against Beijing's transactional approach.

Thus, the Modi administration launched 'Project Mausam' to rival China's Maritime Silk Route (MSR) and naval activities in the IOR to counter the growing Chinese naval activity in the Indian Ocean region. As *Mausam* (Hindi: मौसम) means weather or season in many South and Southeast Asian languages, it highlighted its profound role in cultural exchanges in the region, since maritime trade in ancient times used to depend on seasonal monsoon winds. With India's challenges spreading from its immediate borders to the high seas (and, as explained above, to its vast strategic neighbourhood) it is a project that is still evolving. Cultural dimensions apart, India's efforts to counter the Chinese got a major strategic boost with the rise of interest in the QUAD—a US-led grouping of Australia, Japan, India and the USA—that has made the Chinese rather uneasy, despite assertions by QUAD members that it is not a military alliance against China. As for India, it is likely to see an even further shift in India's strategic focus on its military capabilities to the Indian Ocean, where India still enjoys an edge over China's navy.

Responses to Crisis Abroad

Thousands of Indian migrant workers were living in West Asia. Unexpectedly, their security came under threat, with the rise of the ISIS in northern Iraq in 2014 at the beginning of Mr. Modi's first tenure as PM, when 46 Indian nurses were reported to have been abducted from the Iraqi town of Mosul. India's diplomatic push later led them to be freed and flown back to India. Later, 39 Indian workers, mostly from Punjab, were taken hostage. They too were eventually freed, despite worrying reports about their fate, initially. A similar situation occurred in Libya where many Indian nationals were stranded because of the armed conflict that broke out in the Libyan town of Benghazi, and other parts of the country. The Indian government chartered a flight from Tunisia and brought over 200 nationals back to India. Eventually, about 3,000 or more Indian nationals returned to India.

After the outbreak of aerial attacks by the Saudi Arabia-led coalition on Yemen, Mr. Modi's Government in India launched a massive rescue operation called Op Rahat (meaning Relief), to save hundreds of non-residential Indians located there. In the process, the Indian Navy deployed its frontline ships while the Indian Air Force and Air India's planes were deployed to airlift the stranded Indians and those of other (26) nationalities. The operation was highly successful and received huge acclamation from across the globe as it rescued not only Indians but thousands of foreigners stranded in the war-torn country. Then, there was the swift Indian response to Nepal's devastating earthquake in April 2015 that left thousands of people dead or homeless. However, the biggest and most remarkable rescue operation that Mr. Modi initiated drawing on the skills of many of his ministers was of 22,000 Indian students caught in the fighting in Ukraine in 2022. 'Operation Ganga' was clearly a remarkable achievement, as all but one Indian student was brought back in herculean airlifts from Europe. No other country attempted anything close to it.

The humanitarian crisis apart, the biggest challenge today for India is to counter the Chinese presence everywhere in India's neighbourhood. Though part of the blame can be put on leaders in the neighbourhood making some politically expedient choices by swaying between 'favourites' or who favours their particular agenda, the harsh reality is that those who chose the outsider as their 'benefactor' have got bogged down in debt traps and saddled with white elephant projects by compromising their political autonomy and even tried to hide the loss of their sovereign territory to salami slicing. Now it is time to stem the rot first and then try to reverse it. For that, India's task is thus cut out: to sensitise its many neighbours about promoting mutual interests and managing differences through honest consultation and greater cooperation. They must accept that the way forward lies in promoting deeper economic integration with mutual consensus, as has been India's policy, and for them to shun predatory economics enforced by outside forces. This remains a considerably big challenge for the Modi government.

To sum up, Narendra Modi's foreign policy pace has been remarkable. In the words of an eminent commentator and columnist, Mr. Modi's "whirlwind visits around the globe to stadium-packed appearances abroad, to selfies and bear hugs with business glitterati and world leaders alike, he has left a distinctive mark on the international stage. Not bad for a former chief minister who had little foreign policy experience and whose first national campaign barely mentioned world affairs." As we can see, his drive is far from over.

17

The Amrit Kaal Has Dawned

Satnam Singh Sandhu

When Prime Minister Narendra Modi took over the reins of a country that had been a victim of nepotism for decades, the aspirations of 1.4 billion people in India hung in the balance. Would he deliver or not? How? When? Eight years later, answers abound; questions have well-nigh vanished, vanquished.

Under PM Modi's charismatic guidance, the nation has taken to progress like never before. Days of rampant corruption are passé; the era of 'Amrit Kaal' has dawned. An all-encompassing term, the PM first used it from the ramparts of the historical Red Fort in New Delhi to underline India's roadmap for the next 25 years. He envisioned 'Amrit Kaal' as a time when the rural and urban and the caste and class divide would melt; when technology would seep into each home, and when the government would only be a facilitator in the growth of the masses.

Ever since the PM took over, detractors have risen in hordes, castigated each move he made, admonished each action he took, critiqued each word he spoke, and rebuked each thought he engendered. However, the man moved on, ignoring stray voices, for his vision was not myopic. He envisioned an India of tomorrow—a country that imbibed the meaning of nationhood; a united entity free of biases, progressive and powerful, in letter and spirit.

The moot question is how has the nation transformed under the leadership of this dynamic person? Well, transformation has to be understood at two levels: one physical, the other cerebral. India has witnessed both. Not only has the nation garnered tangible assets in the form of state-of-the-art infrastructure, but the people now think of the country as a secure unit that offers scope for growth for every person. Much is known, but it is time to know more; information dissemination is what the PM aims at.

Let us take up the latter first. How did the masses gain confidence initially? In September 2016, a dastardly 'fidayeen' attack on an army base in Uri, Jammu & Kashmir, rocked the nation. Terrorists from across the border extinguished precious lives; men in olive green were slaughtered. PM Modi did not take it lying down; he responded like none before him had. Just days later, the Indian Army resorted to surgical strikes, pre-emptive steps to crush the enemy and nip the evil in the bud. Our elite troops successfully launched a lethal attack on terror platforms in Pakistan and reduced them to rubble, a step that galvanized the nation. However, there was more to come; the enemy did not rest.

On 14 February 2019, a Central Reserve Police Force (CRPF) convoy was ambushed by a suicide bomber in Pulwama district of the erstwhile state of Jammu and Kashmir. As many as 40 Indian troops were killed in this act of shame. PM Modi once again resorted to strict action, adhering to his 'no-tolerance of terror' approach. This time around, the Indian Air Force was pressed into action and terror bases in Balakot, Pakistan, were smashed to smithereens. In just eight minutes, the Indian Air Force caused havoc in enemy territory; a lesson for them that India would neither cower nor submit.

Wing Commander Abhinandan Varthaman, an Indian Air Force fighter pilot, showcased what new India was all about. With his MiG-21 Bison, he shot down an F-16 new generation aircraft of the enemy. In the process, his plane took a hit and crash-landed in enemy territory. After being held captive for nearly three days, Abhinandan returned to a hero's welcome to be honourably bestowed with a Vir Chakra by the Indian government. An act of bravery that posterity will remember and cherish.

His story was there for the world to witness, but few know about

Squadron Leader Minty Agarwal, who was part of the operation. She guided the brave men and was backing Abhinandan till a jammed communication system led him to the other side of the border. Agarwal was awarded a Yudh Seva Medal for distinguished service on 15 August 2019, becoming the first woman to have received the honour. Women too are soaring high!

This is what the nation is under the PM; a brave, united, group, never wilting under pressure, and willing to make the ultimate sacrifice if the need arises. Did it inspire confidence in the common man? Yes, it did. Now, every child in every nook and corner of the country knows what India is, what the nation stands for and what PM Modi's vision is. Has it ever happened before? No, never!

New India is about this mental transformation, where each citizen is as confident as the government that is backing them. All of us are stakeholders now, unlike never before and the credit goes to the man at the helm—PM Modi.

Moving from external borders, let us talk about how the Prime Minister has galvanized each individual of the country to adopt a positive approach, cultivate a spirit of nationhood and look forward to the future with hope. A transformation in attitude much required to take the nation forward. That is what he has cultivated, that is what he will nurture and that is what will bear fruit in the times to come.

To bind us together, the PM tapped into the sporting spirit of youngsters through the Khelo India Games. Through various initiatives like the Target Olympics Podium Scheme (TOPS) and Mission Olympics Cell, our athletes are slowly but surely climbing the ladder of success, aiming for the top slot and confident of acing their goals. In each town, each village, each district, each panchayat of the country, budding athletes are now dreaming big.

Javelin thrower Neeraj Chopra's gold medal at the Tokyo Olympics is egging them on; ace shuttler P.V. Sindhu's bronze medal is galvanizing them; weightlifter Mirabai Chanu's silver medal is inspiring them to work harder; boxer Lovlina Borgohain's bronze is fuelling their desire; and the hockey team's success and those of the other medallists is setting new goals for them. The time is not far when Indian athletes will outshine all others.

Badminton ace P.V. Sindhu famously shared how the PM offered her ice-cream when he hosted the Indian athletes at his residence after a successful stint at the Tokyo Olympics. Is there a precedent like this? Has the PM of any nation offered an ice-cream to a superlative athlete after her grand success? Highly unlikely!

The BJP government's firm focus is on scouting talent from rural areas and investing in the future of these athletes with state-of-the-art facilities. We will soon be a sporting powerhouse under the able guidance of the PM; 2024 Paris Olympics and 2028 Los Angeles Olympics are the twin goals, and then India is set to host the 2036 Olympics in Ahmedabad. It has never happened before, and this is a modicum of what is to come in the future.

A man of PM Modi's vision knows that if the nation is fit, the future belongs to Indians. Our numbers are an asset; it is about time to make them count. Is that not a transformation? Few would doubt this.

Now let us get to the physical transformation of India. Here statistics abound. Let us look at some. Our poverty rate has been reduced from 22 per cent to 10 per cent, while the per capita income has doubled and so have our foreign reserves. Only 637,000 primary schools were constructed in the country in the past seven decades, but under PM Modi's government, 653,000 schools have already been built so far and the process continues.

In the health sector, 15 new All-India Institutes of Medical Sciences have been sanctioned; ten are already operational and five are ready to take off. As many as 1.2 million doctors have entered the service of the nation. We now have the second largest road network in the world, while solar and wind power generation capacity has been doubled.

'Sabka Saath, Sabka Vikas, Sabka Vishwas, Sabka Prayas', is the mantra that the PM abides by. Each one of us together, progressing, building trust and making efforts for an India that is entering the 'Amrit Kaal' phase, where an aspirational society will ace each goal and fulfil each dream. In 2047, India will be celebrating a hundred years of its independence, so the next 25 years belong to us, to the PM's vision and an era of prosperity.

The 'Amrit Kaal' philosophy stands on four pillars: Brightening the lives of Indian citizens, bridging the gap between rural and urban India, making the government a facilitator and bringing about the dawning of an era of cutting-edge technology. Who has ever thought of this before?

Was not the handling of the COVID-19 crisis in the country a definitive example of Amrit Kaal? How were 1.41 billion people vaccinated? How was data accurately available on the CoWIN app? From our house help to us, to everybody we met, everyone was vaccinated, and the data was there for everyone to see. Is this not transformation?

Was not technology pressed into action at each step, the fourth pillar of Amrit Kaal? If there are questions and smirking from the so-called intelligentsia, let them rest in peace. It is time, right? No government could have achieved this feat, none ever faced a pandemic. None ever encountered a crisis even one-fourth the magnitude of this one. So, are we transforming? A firm 'yes' should be the answer.

Let us go back to data again; statistics speak for themselves.

Food grain production in the country has gone up from 255 million tonnes in 2012-13 to 316.06 million tonnes in 2021-22, a record the present BJP government can wear as a badge of honour. Food and energy security is the common man's concern, and PM Modi is securing it with each step he takes.

A look at the schemes offered under his aegis, and only the names would suffice: Ayushman Bharat Yojana, Kisan Samman Nidhi, Jan Dhan Yojana, Ujjwala Yojana, Kisan Samman Nidhi, Ayushman Bharat Yojana, Gareeb Kalyan Yojana, Swachh Bharat Yojana, Awas Yojana, Jal Jivan Mission, Atmanirbhar Bharat, Vocal for Local, Gati Shakti Yojana, PLI (production-linked incentive), in fact many more. For physical transformation of the nation, this should be sufficient.

There is more than just statistics though.

The scrapping of Article 370, construction of the grand Ram Temple in Ayodhya, abolition of Triple Talaq, passing of the Citizenship Amendment Act; identification of 1,800 redundant laws and the scrapping of 1,450. What else is there to prove? From here on, only Amrit Kaal is being ushered.

As for foreign policy, the nation is forging strong ties with countries across the globe without compromising on any of its principles, without taking sides, without appeasing, without bending. Since PM Modi assumed office, things have been fast forwarded as he has made the country a strategic player on the international stage.

While India has traditionally been non-aligned in its approach, now we have a robust foreign policy that seeks to stamp its identity on global forums and make the world acknowledge it. The zero-tolerance approach towards terrorism has strengthened our core and united each individual against perpetrators of terror. Dynamic, vibrant and prophetic, our foreign policy goals are much clearer than ever before, even as we move into a multi-polar world. No longer are we bystanders on the world stage; we are actively forging global alliances and fashioning them for others as well.

Malleability is another highlight of India's foreign policy, but the interests of the nation are of prime importance. Our measured approach to the Russian invasion of Ukraine defines that in ample measure. While the West wanted to dictate its terms, India stood firm, called for a diplomatic solution to the whole crisis and even purchased Russian crude oil at a discounted price, which makes perfect economic sense.

Climate change is another sphere on which the PM is deeply focused. He has pledged that the country's emissions would be reduced to zero by 2070. On the wings of renewable sources of energy, he wants to reduce our carbon footprints and build a future where energy security is achieved. Self-interest is what the West thinks of our foreign policy. We take pride in that, we always will. Under the able guidance of a dynamic leader like PM Modi, there is no retracing. Each step surges ahead with confidence.

Recently, the G-20 summit in Bali marked a watershed. PM Modi received the G-20 presidency from the Indonesian president at the closing ceremony of the summit. From 1 December 2022, India assumed office and aims at an inclusive partnership with all nations on board. It is decisive action, goal-oriented. Has it ever happened before?

On the sidelines of the summit, within hours of PM Modi meeting the newly-elected British Prime Minister of Indian origin, Rishi Sunak, UK cleared 3,000 visas for Indians. There is more to come. This is just the beginning.

Coming back to transformation on the personal level, the 'Har Ghar Tiranga' campaign under the Azadi Ka Amrit Mahotsav marked the 75th year of India's independence. A first-of-its kind initiative by PM Modi, the move made every Indian's relationship with the Tricolour more personal than institutional. The national flag on each house fluttered with pride, signifying our commitment to the cause of nation-building, evoking a spirit of patriotism.

The PM's will and the willingness of 1.41 billon people of India will make us a formidable force to reckon with in the future. Time is on our side, and so is world opinion. Should we surge ahead? Yes! Can anyone stop us? No!

18

NEP 2020: Foundation for Stability

Shishir Bajoria

A nation's strength is its people and the people's strength is education. Education is much more than a degree. It should impart knowledge, skill and prepare the young mind to face the world with courage and determination. Blind pursuit of a degree over the years has made us a country which has the highest number of educated unemployed force while, on the other hand, a big shortage of employable people. Unfortunately, there are no established platforms for dialogue between academia and industry, trade and commerce, which results in us producing square pegs to fill round holes.

Educated unemployed, especially among the youngest in the country, is very dangerous. After going through tremendous pressure and a gruelling journey in pursuit of a degree and not getting gainful employment has all the ingredients for youth taking to counter-productive measures. Parental and peer pressure reaches such a crescendo that many a student commits suicide for the fear of either not being successful or in some cases for not achieving the highest marks. Unfortunately, till recently, our education policy had no connect with life after getting a degree.

In the last eight years, the Prime Minister Narendra Modi-led government has brought radical reforms in the primary and higher education system in the country. The 34–year-old education policy has been replaced by the

National Education Policy, 2020. The changes that the NEP is bringing will completely transform the way we look at education. Internationalization of higher education, while staying grounded in history, culture and the ethos of India is another aspect that this government is seriously looking into. It is, therefore, important that we discuss and analyze the measures taken by the government and show how India is striving to be a force to be reckoned with in the education sector.

National Education Policy (NEP), 2020

Quality education and infrastructure is at the core of our constitutional promises of social and economic justice and equality of opportunity. It strives to transform the manner and methods of disseminating knowledge and skills to equip our young citizens to compete globally. The global education development agenda reflected in Goal 4 (SDG4) of the 2030 Agenda for Sustainable Development, adopted by India in 2015, seeks to "ensure inclusive and equitable quality education and promote lifelong learning opportunities for all" by 2030. The NEP is a step towards that goal by having the entire education system to be reconfigured to support and foster learning, so that all the critical targets and goals (SDGs) of the 2030 Agenda for Sustainable Development can be achieved.

The NEP envisaged pedagogy from a different prism—that education ought to be experiential, multidisciplinary, integrated and inquiry-driven to promote innovation and critical thinking in new fields. Therefore, the curriculum must be such that it makes education more well-rounded, useful, and fulfilling to the learner.

India's rich and timeless knowledge bank through civilization inspires the new outlook to education that is the NEP. The policy document notes that '*the pursuit of knowledge (Gyan), wisdom (Pragyaa), and truth (Satya) was always considered in Indian thought and philosophy as the highest human goal. The aim of education in ancient India was not just the acquisition of knowledge as preparation for life in this world, or life beyond schooling, but for the complete realization and liberation of the self.*'

India was the epicentre of a multidisciplinary education that hosted scholars and leaders of the world who documented India's thought leadership;

some of these world-class institutions of ancient India were Takshashila, Nalanda, Vikramshila, Vallabhi, among others. The New Education Policy duly recognizes that '*the Indian education system produced great scholars such as Charaka, Susruta, Aryabhata, Varahamihira, Bhaskaracharya, Brahmagupta, Chanakya, Chakrapani Datta, Madhava, Panini, Patanjali, Nagarjuna, Gautama, Pingala, Sankardev, Maitreyi, Gargi and Thiruvalluvar, among numerous others, who made seminal contributions to world knowledge in diverse fields such as mathematics, astronomy, metallurgy, medical science and surgery, civil engineering, architecture, shipbuilding and navigation, yoga, fine arts, chess, and more.*' Nurturing and formulating the future of education from unparalleled elements of our past is integral to the methods devised under the NEP.

Reimagining School Education

The foremost reform is the change from a 10+2 years education system at the school level to a 5+3+3+4 system. The first part of this is early education and child care, which is critical since over 85 per cent of a child's brain development takes place before six years of age. For this, a National Curricular and Pedagogical Framework for Early Childhood Care and Education (NCPFECCE) for children up to eight years of age will be developed by NCERT. This will involve upgradation of the Anganwadi system where workers will be given a certificate programme on many aspects of literacy, numeracy and cognitive development for engagement with toddlers.

The aim of achieving universal foundational literacy by 2025 is fundamental to the NEP. This entails a National Mission on Foundational Literacy and Numeracy to ensure complete coverage in the most basic tasks of reading, writing and numeracy. For this, the NEP aims at a pupil-teacher ratio (PTR) of 30:1 and in areas of socio-economic disadvantage a PTR of 25:1, matching global standards. Besides the curriculum on ECCE, it also envisages a national repository of high-quality resources on foundational literacy and numeracy known as Digital Infrastructure for Knowledge Sharing (DIKSHA) which is a one-of-a-kind repository with universal access that will allow easy access to useful resources in every household through low-end smart phones as well as community service centres.

The NEP also focuses on a multidisciplinary and flexible approach in that there are no strict bounds between curricular, co-curricular and extra-curricular. It allows for holistic planning wherein providing freedom and choice is at the core of an individual's development. A student can have arts, vocational skills, sciences and mathematics, for instance.

It is well understood that at an early stage, the ability to grasp ideas and grow cognitive ability is best done in one's mother tongue. The NEP allows for multilingualism as a means of quality education. The three-language formula has laid emphasis on a holistic approach to education. This ordinarily means learning in one's mother tongue/regional language along with English and the third language could be among other Indian languages or from a selection of foreign languages depending on the choice of the state, the students and the provision by schools. Therefore, it allows for students to learn organically in their own language, have global proficiency through English as well as learn another Indian language that will enhance social and political integration. The issue of language imposition is misconceived since the NEP does not take away from the local/regional/state language and also does not specify or favour any particular Indian language as a third language. In the past, it has been seen that state governments, to gain populism, took kneejerk actions only to reverse it after a few years. However, during this period, countless futures were adversely impacted.

From an infrastructure point of view, the NEP seeks to transform the primary schools as a geographical unit as it is seen that under the Sarva Shiksha Abhiyan about 15 per cent of upper primary schools and 28 per cent of primary schools have less than 30 students which make them financially and operationally unviable to run, becoming a burden on scarce state finances and human resource while causing children to lose out for lack of access. Therefore, the NEP envisages the creation of school complexes with integrated infrastructure for curricular education, arts, sports and vocational skills.

Making Higher Education Viable and Globally Competitive

The NEP has also fundamentally changed the Indian outlook to higher education which had seen compartmentalization in silos that reflected an outdated structure of higher education. Primary among these reforms is the immense flexibility in structuring of courses both in substance and time. Undergraduate degrees of three or four years will have multiple exit options with appropriate recognition—a certificate after completing one year of study, a diploma after completing two years of study, and a Bachelor's after three years of study with a 'with research degree' if completed with a research project in the fourth year.

This innovative structuring of higher education is the right fit for an emerging economy on a multi-year growth cycle that needs trained human capital in the millions every year. It allows access to education without the prohibitive opportunity cost for students with low-income backgrounds who can now opt to be part of the workforce with a certification or a diploma in professional/vocational courses. This is also in sync with the increasing demand of the specialized nature of employment needed in industry, especially in areas where India is seeking to position itself as a global alternative such as the defence manufacturing or semiconductors industry.

A similar perspective has been brought to the Master's programme where a two-year degree will follow a three-year Bachelor programme, or a one-year Master's with a four-year Bachelor programme or an integrated five-year Bachelor/Master programme.

The programmes will be structured in a manner to focus on research and foster innovative and quality output in incubation centres, technology development centres, interdisciplinary research such as in epidemiology and diagnostics, physics, neurobiology, etc., and have better industry linkages. Institutions will have freedom to structure courses and pedagogy to stimulate learning and research.

Impetus to Vocational Education

The 12th Five Year Plan estimates that less than 5 per cent of the workforce within the age of 19-24 have formal vocational education. In comparison, USA has 52 per cent, Germany 75 per cent and South Korea 96 per cent. In a multi-polar world looking at diversified supply chains, India needs consistently higher levels of vocational training to grab the opportunity of being the world's growth engine.

For this, the NEP envisages exposure to vocational skills from an early age rather than only post-school. It is also planned to integrate secondary schools with ITIs, polytechnics and skill labs created in a hub-and-spoke model to create adequate access and industry opportunity in a structured manner such that vocational education is taken as a serious and viable option by households.

Digitizing Education

On the digital front, the success of the Modi government has been remarkable. Through its flagship programme, the Digital India Campaign, efforts are being taken to improve the digital infrastructure in the country. The Education Ministry initiated the National Digital Library of India to provide a virtual repository of resources provided to students without any cost.

SWAYAM (Study Webs of Active–Learning for Young Aspiring Minds) portal was established to provide quality education to the most disadvantaged groups of the country. It provides free open online courses to students on a variety of subjects and evaluation is also done every semester to check the progress. For students who do not have access to online education, the Budget 2022 pledged one class one channel for each of 12 classes through SWAYAM Prabha.

DIKSHA (Digital Infrastructure for Knowledge Sharing) portal was formed in 2017 to promote remote school education and as a digital infrastructure for teachers and students. The portal provides quality e-content as well as QR codes textbooks.

The National Testing Agency (NTA) was formed to conduct entrance exams for admission to higher education making the process quicker and more transparent.

The Government has also announced the formation of a Digital University in Budget 2022-23 in order to solve the problem of limited seats in higher education institutions.

Nari Shakti in Education

The Government has also taken steps for the promotion of education of the girl child. In 2015, it launched the 'Beti Bachao Beti Padhao' initiative which focuses on challenging the patriarchal mindset of the people of the country and advancing the education of girls. The gross enrolment of the girl child has increased to 52 per cent from 39 per cent in 2020 in Higher Secondary. There has also been relatively fewer dropouts among girl students.

Separate toilets for the girls have been built so that they can easily attend school. In 2020, 97 per cent schools were covered, up from 89 per cent in 2013, and efforts are being taken so that every school has separate toilets for girls.

UDAAN initiative was taken by the CBSE to enable girl students to transit from school education to professional education by providing free online resources for preparation. The Department of Science and Technology launched KIRAN (Knowledge Involvement in Research Advancement through Nurturing) scheme to promote women in the field of science and bridge the gender gap in the sector by providing them with fellowships.

The government introduced supernumerary seats for women for admission in IITs in 2018 at 14 per cent which was later increased to 20 per cent. Five years on, in the latest admission cycle in 2022-23, all the 20 per cent seats, that is 3,310 girls out of 16,635 seats have been admitted to IITs.

IITs, IIMs, Medical and Higher Education

The Government has taken considerable efforts to increase the access of higher education in the country. Since 2014, the number of IITs has been increased from 16 to 23 and IIMs from 13 to 20 increasing the seat count from around 3,500 in 2014 to over 5,500 in 2022.

The Modi Government has set up a new university every week and two new colleges have come up every day since 2014. This has resulted in a significant progress in the number of students getting higher education in the country. The total number of students in higher education has increased from 3.45 crore in 2015 to 3.85 crore in 2020.

The government has also doubled the number of AIIMSs, many of which have already been established or are in the process of starting. In the last seven years, the number of medical colleges has increased to 596 from 387 in 2014. The seats in these colleges have also been increased from 82,000 to 1.48 lakh seats.

The government has laid primary focus on the often-neglected regions of India. In seven years, it established the first central university in Ladakh and 22 new universities in Northeast India. What is remarkable is that India has also set up its first ever forensic university and rail and transport university under the present government.

Three Indian universities, namely, IIT Bombay, IIT Delhi and IISc Bengaluru, have been ranked amongst the top 200 universities in the world in the QS World University Rankings 2021 and a record 71 Indian universities have made it to the Times Higher Education World University Rankings in 2021.

To improve the higher education infrastructure in the country, the government launched the RISE scheme. The scheme is being implemented by the Higher Education Financial Agency (HEFA). The government increased the capital base from 10,000 crore to 1 lakh crore.

It is undeniable that in ancient times India was a world leader in terms of education and the knowledge system. Hundreds of years of invasions and plunders made the country shift its focus from education to other areas essential to life and livelihood. We are now in a position, financially, to recalibrate our energy again into making India a knowledge powerhouse by implementing radical changes in the education sector and making it at par with international standards. The last eight years of the Modi government have been instrumental in and testimony to the new era of education reforms that the country is heralding.

19

INDIA'S DISASTER RESPONSE AND RESILIENCE

R K Pachnanda

India is vulnerable, in varying degrees, to a large number of disasters. Over 58.6 per cent of the landmass is prone to earthquakes. Over 12 per cent of land is prone to floods and river erosion. Close to 5,700 kilometres, out of the 7,516 kilometres long coastline, is prone to cyclones and tsunamis. 68 per cent of cultivable area is vulnerable to droughts. Hilly areas are at risk from landslides and avalanches. Around 6 per cent of the population of India is impacted annually by the exposures to disasters. The key natural disasters in India include floods, droughts, cyclones, earthquakes, landslides, avalanches and fires that have resulted in loss of lives and livelihood. The spectre of disaster or emergencies of chemical, biological and nuclear (CBRN) origin has increased. Industrial and chemical disasters can occur due to accidents or negligence and can result in huge loss to lives and property.

Earlier, we had no real set up to respond to disaster. While India was celebrating Republic Day 2001, a monster earthquake shook the Kutch area of eastern Gujarat causing massive devastation. The tremor lasted for just two minutes but left nearly 20,000 people dead and around 1,67,000 injured with over a million structures destroyed. The ancient city of Bhuj was flattened. This earthquake changed India's response to disaster. The herculean reconstruction efforts put in by the then Chief Minister, Gujarat, Narendra

Modi helped rebuild the state. To contain the enormity of future calamities, the state made disaster risk protection its priority and set up institutions like the Gujarat State Disaster Management Authority (GSDMA), the Institute of Seismological Research (ISI) and Gujarat Institute of Disaster Management (GIDM). A round the clock network of over 60 seismic stations was set up to measure tremors, 50 of which were located in the Kutch region alone and now the threat of an earthquake can be determined in less than two minutes and alert sent in less than l0 minutes. The state augmented its fire services; GSDMA developed the hazard risk vulnerability atlas, the first of its kind in the country to assess the vulnerability of six different kinds of disasters i.e. earthquake, tsunamis, floods, cyclones, droughts and chemical and industrial hazards.

In a short period of time, Gujarat became one of the least risk investment destinations in the country in terms of disaster preparedness. The Gujarat model of disaster preparedness served as a paradigm for building a national response to variegated calamities. Learning from previous disasters, the government crafted a multi-dimensional and multi sector approach by taking measures to strengthen the legal, financial and institutional mechanisms for disaster risk reduction and to build capacity for response, relief, reconstruction and recovery across sectors.

India was quick to adopt and align its priorities with a Hygo framework for action that re-emphasizes the need to build resilience of the community to disasters. The National Disaster Management Act was enacted in 2005 and the National Disaster Management Authority was formed. A National Disaster Response Force (NDRF) was formed in 2006 with 12 Battalions and 23 Regional Response Centres stationed across the country. This, purely, humanitarian force has, over the years, responded most promptly and professionally to disasters and in saving lives and livelihood and India is perhaps the only country to have such a dedicated force to handle calamities.

For any country to respond effectively to natural disaster, its early warning systems, information management and weather forecasting are important and these were evolved by the Indian National Centre for Ocean Information Service which provides early warnings through 300 metrological stations; it has been sending constant alerts and advisory services. The Indian

Metrological department has revolutionized the weather monitoring process with the help of remote sensing techniques. Buoys in the tropical oceans and satellites integrated automated weather stations have been installed for accurate forecasting and timely detection and warning communication and response. The Indian Space Research Organization (ISRO) has evolved a comprehensive space base disaster management system which will have multiple applications including risk management and early warning systems for the region. Community based disaster risk management programmes for millions of people residing in remote and highly risk areas to tackle the onslaught of calamities have been organized leading to a transformational reduction in loss of life. The same trigger has been applied at national, state and district levels for governments and civil society groups to prepare communities for disasters. Vulnerable public buildings have been retrofitted and evacuation plans are in place with a mission to reduce losses of property and lives. The National Disaster Management Authority (NDMA) has done Yeoman's work on all aspects and has coordinated the enforcement and implementation of the policy and plans of disaster management very effectively.

The measures undertaken over the years brought successful results which were seen when the disaster prone Odisha was hit by "Hudhud" cyclone in 2015 and the loss of lives came down from over 10,000 to two digit figures.

It is a matter of great pride for India that the Prime Minister took the initiative and responded promptly to the earthquake in Nepal by extending immediate help and resources. NDRF was the first international rescue force to arrive along with the Nepalese Forces. It worked tirelessly to retrieve both live victims and the dead from the debris and helped rescue 11 out of the 16 victims alive and brought out 133 dead from the debris. NDRF was also rushed to Turkey and rescued two girls alive and retrieved 78 bodies in "Operation Dost".

Today, the NDRF has developed itself into a highly professional force. During disaster, the NDRF responds immediately to save lives in the earth quakes, cyclones, floods etc. In situations of impending disasters, NDRF teams are prepositioned in advance to handle any contingency. For example, in Cyclone Vardah in Tamil Nadu and Andhra Pradesh, NDRF teams were prepositioned, well in advance, and, immediately, after the landfall, cleared 3000 trees and 190 kms of roads in just 2 days in a blitz-krieg operation and restored electric poles to bring immediate normalcy in the situation. In periods when there is no disaster, the NDRF unflinchingly strives by sensitizing and preparing communities in disaster resilience and disaster risk reduction through National Capacity Building Programmes. These include Community Awareness Programmes, School Safety Programmes, Mock Drills, etc. So far, NDRF has trained more than 65 lakh people in these Community Capacity Building Programmes in the country. The NDRF is also tirelessly training State level forces like SDRFs and holding joint mock drill regularly. NDRF works in close coordination with stake holders. The number of capacity building exercise and mock drills have increased and the object is that the community should act as a force multiplier. The response time of NDRF has greatly improved. And it is response which is the crucial element to saving lives. NDRF has rescued over 1.48 lakh precious lives and evacuated over 7 lakh persons stranded in disaster situations in India and abroad.

In order to make the country disaster resilient, the Prime Minister unveiled a National Disaster Management Plan that is aligned to the Sendai framework. In the Asia Pacific region, India has taken the lead on several fronts. In 2015, it organized the South Asian Annual Disaster Management Exercise, SADMEX, for all the SAARC member countries, with the focus to test inter-governmental coordination and create synergy to synchronize efforts to institutionalize regional cooperation on disaster response. It was followed by the SAARC Regional Workshop on sharing best practices. In August 2016, India hosted the meeting of BRICS Ministers for Disaster Management where it was agreed to set up a Joint Task Force on Disaster Risk Management for regular dialogue, exchange, mutual support and collaboration among BRICS countries. In November 2016, the Government of India hosted the Asian Ministerial Conference on Disaster Risk Reduction. The theme was "Risk Sensitive Development for Community Resilience". The object was discussing strengthening community resilience, risk resilient critical infrastructure, implementing the health aspects of Sendai framework, promoting educational continuity and resilience of children and communities, disaster risk identification and financing solutions, etc. The Conference concluded with (i) a Political Declaration, reaffirming the government and stakeholders' commitment to Disaster Risk Reduction, and (ii) adoption of the Regional Plan for implementation of the Sendai Framework for Disaster Risk Reduction. At this conference, the Government of India and United Nations Office for Disaster Risk Reduction (UNIDSR) signed a statement underlining the guiding principles towards effective implementation and monitoring of the Sendai Framework on Disaster Risk Reduction.

It was at this Conference that the Prime Minister of India unveiled the l0 point Agenda on Disaster Risk Reduction and proposed to set up a "Coalition on Disaster Resilient Infrastructure (CDRI)" among the partner countries, which goes as follows:

1. All development sectors must imbibe the principles of disaster risk management.
2. Work towards risk coverage for all-starting from poor households to SMEs to multinational corporations to nation states.
3. Encourage greater involvement and leadership of women in disaster risk management.
4. Invest in risk mapping globally. For mapping risks related to hazards like earthquakes, we have accepted standards and parameters.
5. Leverage technology to enhance the efficiency of our disaster risk management efforts.
6. Develop a network of universities to work on disaster issues.
7. Utilize the opportunities provided by social media and mobile technologies.
8. Build on local capacity and initiatives.
9. Opportunities to learn from a disaster must not be wasted. After every disaster there are papers on lessons that are rarely applied.
10. Bring about greater cohesion in international response to disasters.

In October 2017, India hosted the first annual Disaster Management Exercise for the Bay of Bengal Initiative for Multi-sectoral, Technical and Economic Co-operation (BIMSTEC) countries for sharing best practices and experience involving their response teams in the form of table top and field exercises. In March 2018, the Government of India organized the first Indo-Japan Workshop on Disaster Risk Reduction in Delhi which was attended by 150 domain experts from India and Japan. The workshop deliberated on various themes viz. disaster management policy framework, risk assessment, disaster resilient infrastructure, early warning system preparedness by sub-national governments and approaches by the private sector. The 2nd Indo-Japan Workshop on Disaster Risk Reduction was held back-to-back with the National Conference for promoting Disaster Risk Reduction (NCPDRR) in October, 2018, in Tokyo. The theme of the workshop was "Preparing for large-scale disasters strengthening a network of collaboration in a community". The 3rd Indo-Japan workshop on Disaster Risk Reduction was held in 2019 in New Delhi. The objective of the workshop was enhancing collaboration between research institutes, cities and the private sector in the field of Disaster Risk Reduction. The International Workshop on Disaster Resilience Infrastructure was held in Delhi in March 2019 and delegates and experts from 33 countries, multilateral development banks, the U.N., the private sector, academics and representatives of Central and State Governments attended the event. Deliberations were held on best global practices prevailing in the resilient infrastructure, key challenges and gaps in existing practices, potential areas for collaboration. The Joint Urban Earthquake Search and Rescue Exercise of SCO Member States was held from in November, 2019 and tenth Meeting of the Heads of departments of Disaster Prevention of SCO Member States in November, 2019. In February 2020, India hosted the 2nd BIMSTEC Disaster Management Exercise in Puri. The 2022 Asia Pacific Ministerial Conference on Disaster Risk Reduction gave an opportunity to share experiences, action and innovation to build a resilient future.

Under PMs' vision for the NPDRR (National Platform for Disaster Risk Reduction), held in New Delhi, in March 2023, disaster risk reduction and management are turning into a mass movement. The PMs priorities emphasise the need for building local capacities and initiative and, especially, women's leadership in disaster management, in line with the PM's 10 point agenda above and the Sendai framework.

The challenges in any emergency response are geo-climatic changes, increase frequency and magnitude of disasters, new challenges in the form of urban flooding/bore-well issues/colliery collapse/forest fires, uncontrolled urban development, rapid industrialization leading to chemical/ radiological accidents and growing deforestation/environmental degradation.

India has done very well in the last eight years, to set the way forward by:

- Strengthening early warning systems.
- Proper vulnerability mapping.
- Preparing and sensitizing the communities as a force multiplier.
- Enforcing bye-laws in building safety.
- Inclusion of Disaster Response/Disaster Risk Deduction/Disaster Management in school curriculums.
- Capacity building to rescue animals in disasters.
- Standard Operating Procedures for differently abled persons.
- Planting trees.
- To follow good practices of other response forces.

2019 witnessed the worst disaster of all – the COVID-19 Pandemic – which attacked the world like a storm. Here too, Prime Minister Modi proved to be a glowing example for the world to emulate. Our visionary Prime Minister exhibited the epitome of inspiration, wisdom and sterling leadership in this most trying, challenging and unprecedented catastrophe. With total control of the country's response mechanism, the patriotic and deft manner in which the Prime Minister took on this challenge, with an unflinching resolve, is unparalleled. And India has tackled the worst attack on the world with aplomb, since our prompt, preventive and pre-emptive response to the foray by this invisible viral adversary helped us counter the onslaught aptly. Even after three waves of COVID-19, India managed to save more lives than most countries of the world. We had one of the lowest fatality rates and highest recovery rates in the world.

In the battle against coronavirus, many democracies used authoritarian and emergency measures and also called in the military, on the streets, to implement restrictions. It is to the great credit of the prime Minister that he has neither invoked any emergency powers nor resorted to authoritarian measures, but proved to be a torchbearer of democracy by taking the support of "We the people of India..." as enshrined in the preamble, which he quoted in his broadcast to the nation. He has reposed his entire trust in 138 crore

Indians by involving each one them as equal and voluntary stakeholders in the fight against coronavirus – at the same time respecting the rule of law and human right of the citizens.

It was only due to the Prime Minister's vision of an Atmanirbhar Bharat that we developed our indigenous vaccine program for countering COVID and India had the largest immunisation drive in the world. We, again, as a true dependable friend, acted as the "pharmacy of the world" and sent vaccines and medical supplies to many countries. And today, we are well prepared, medically, to counter any such calamity.

Prime Minister Modi has, with unflinching resolve, ensured that India has become a voice and a leader amongst partner nations in unfolding a safer future. With his untiring initiative, it is obvious that under the leadership of Prime Minister Narendra Modi, India, the world's second most populous country, is ever prepared by building a sustainable and resilient system and by integrating disaster risk reduction in its development planning.

INDEX